STUBB'S
BAR-B-Q
COOKBOOK

To Elaine and Robert
on the occasion of
your marriage. May
you have many years
together and many grilling
opportunities. Love,
Mary Kay Beck
Aug. 6, 2011

from

STUBB'S LEGENDARY

KITCHEN

BICENTENNIAL
BICENTENNIAL
1807
WILEY
2007
BICENTENNIAL
BICENTENNIAL

JOHN WILEY & SONS, INC.

THE STUBB'S BAR-B-Q COOKBOOK

with Kate Heyhoe

Photography by Alexandra Grablewski

Copyright © 2007 by One World Foods Inc., dba Stubb's Legendary Kitchen. All rights reserved

Photography copyright © 2007 by Alexandr Grablewski
Food styling by Megan Fawn Schlow
Prop styling by Leslie Siegel

Published by John Wiley & Sons, Inc., Hoboken, New Jersey

Published simultaneously in Canada

For general information on our other products and services or for technical support, please contact our Customer Care Department within the United States at (800) 762-2974, outside the United States at (317) 572-3993 or fax (317) 572-4002.

Wiley also publishes its books in a variety of electronic formats. Some content that appears in print may not be available in electronic books. For more information about Wiley products, visit our web site at www.wiley.com.

Library of Congress Cataloging-in-Publication Data:

Stubblefield, C. B., 1931-
    The Stubb's bar-b-q cookbook : from Stubb's legendary kitchen with Kate Heyhoe.
        p. cm.
    Includes index.
    ISBN: 978-0-471-97996-8 (cloth)
    1. Barbecue cookery. 2. Cookery--Texas. 3. Stubblefield, C. B., 1931–
I. Heyhoe, Kate. II. Title.

    TX840.B3S772 2007
    641.7'6--dc22

                                                                                2006026716

Designed by Cassandra J. Pappas

Photo Credits: Pages vi, xx, 65: Alan Messer © Stubbs Collection; pages viii, xii, 1, 21, 59, 74: © Stubbs Collection; pages 9, 43: © Paul Milosevich; page 99: Neal J. Menschel, Staff © *Christian Science Monitor*; page 106: © Milton Adams; page xi: Numbered clockwise from top-left: #1 © Terry Allen; #2 © Paul Milosevich; #3, #4, #5, #6, and #8 © Stubb's Collection; #7 © Sharon Ely

Printed in China

10 9 8 7 6 5 4 3 2 1

⟶➤ Contents

—•≫ Introduction

My Life Is in These Bottles

> "Barbecue is eternal, like the Mississippi River. It's big and
> it's simple and it takes its own sweet time."
>
> —*C. B. "Stubb" Stubblefield*

A West Texas hero with hands the size of briskets, Stubb didn't just make barbecue. He made friends. His wide, trademark grin roped anyone into the spirit of the moment, whether it was singing the blues or savoring his smoke-scented brisket, slaw, and beans.

A tree of a man, Stubb stood tall at 6'4". He worked the pit in barbecue-splattered overalls, shaded by a cowboy hat. For fancy occasions, he donned boots, jeans, pearl-snapped shirts, a Levi jacket, and a jet black Stetson. His hat was as natural an appendage as his long, strong arms. Even David Letterman remarked, "When was the last time you took that thing off?"

C. B. Stubblefield grew up pickin' cotton. His father was a preacher and sharecropper, and his mother tended to their twelve children. From his father's sermons, Stubb learned about love, compassion, caring, and sharing, and throughout his life, he'd give money or food to anyone who needed it, even if he needed it more.

Like West Texas oil through a rusty pipe, Stubb's deep, resonant drawl flowed thick, slow, and smooth. When he told stories, he could be—much like his preacher father—both laconic and long winded at the same time. He picked words that were economical and to the point, but once started, he'd dramatically drag a story, or a song, on endlessly, yet never for a second lose the attention of his listeners.

Stubb had the talent and the drive to make people happy. Even in the army, in Korea, feeding the troops on barbecue, chili, and homemade Texas blues seemed to be in his blood. But back home, Stubb was just another soldier looking for a new life to live.

It all came together in Lubbock, Texas, at a white stucco building, with platters of barbecue and beaucoups of blues. Local musicians made it their home and hotspot, and soon Muddy Waters, Willie Nelson, George Thorogood, and other recording artists discovered that Stubb's was *the* place to be.

But whether he was cooking for Johnny Cash or President Jimmy Carter, Stubb *always*—like the mighty Mississippi—took his own sweet time. He never rushed the pit, or the sauce. Time, and plenty of it, was Stubb's path for creating truly great barbecue.

At the request of friends, Stubb bottled his first sauce in jam jars and whiskey bottles in 1989, and before long, they and their friends were asking for more. Today, Stubb lives on in his sauces and rubs, continuing to make people feel good all over the world.

For folks who knew him, Stubb was a hero and a living legend. Now, in these recipes and recollections, you too can see why Stubb grew to be so liked and so loved.

As Stubb said, "My life is in these bottles." Here's a taste of what that very special life was all about.

Stubb's Story: "Ladies and Gentlemen, I'm a Cook"

C. B. Stubblefield, better known as Stubb, was one of 12 children born to a brush arbor preacher and his wife. He was, as his mother said, "born hungry" on March 7, 1931, in Navasota, a small town on the Brazos River, in the East Texas cotton belt.

Growing Up

Preacher Stubblefield had a knack for bringing folks together with uplifting music, inspirational stories, and plates of barbecue—much as his son C. B. would do later in life. He preached under trees or tents, fueling his congregation on potluck dinners of beef, pork, and even raccoon and possum. Occasionally, hand-shelled pecans were baked into pies, and sometimes a buttermilk pie would show up, sweet and golden brown.

Stubb and his family picked cotton to the steady beat of "East Texas blues," music spun from work songs and delta harmonies. The area's most famous musicians—Lightnin' Hopkins, Blind Lemon Jefferson, and T-Bone Walker—would later spin their unique style of blues on a vintage jukebox at Stubb's Bar-B-Que, and some would even play there live.

When Stubb turned 13, the Stubblefields headed northwest to the cotton fields of Lubbock. West Texas has always been an unexpected incubator of musical talent. It's the birthplace of rock 'n' roll legend Buddy Holly, and other musicians, including Joe Ely, Jimmie Dale Gilmore, and Butch Hancock (collectively known as the Flatlanders), Waylon Jennings, Bob Wills, Jesse "Guitar" Taylor, the Gatlin Brothers, Jimmy Dean, Mac Davis, Terry Allen, Kimmie Rhodes, and Lloyd Maines and his Dixie Chicks daughter, Natalie Maines. In a ramshackle restaurant in a dry and dusty town, Stubb would one day change the lives of many of these artists, and they would do the same for him.

Stubb married a woman who was as short as he was tall, but the two were equally matched in strength of character. "Is you is, or is you ain't, gonna be my wife?" he asked, with his irresistible grin. Cleola Ruth was a few years older than Stubb, with four children from a previous marriage. In fact, Stubb was but eight years older than her own son, and only 17 years old himself when he proposed to Cleo.

Stubb and Cleo raised two children of their own. Their first daughter died in Stubb's arms, when she was six months old, of pneumonia. Doris Jean was born a few months later, in 1949, and their son, Christopher, came along in 1953. "Because Daddy never went far in school, we kids *had* to be educated," says Doris. "Some parents took their children out of school to pick cotton. But not us. Daddy would have had a fit! We'd eat beans or rice or whatever to make ends meet, but we never missed school—not even one day."

The Army Years

In Lubbock, C. B. Stubblefield and his family became accustomed to "makin' do with what you got." Everyone worked whatever odd jobs they could, often in restaurants. Stubb showed a special flair for cooking, and in the U.S. Army, Stubb got his first chance to feed thousands.

Stubb was first assigned to the 96th Field Artillery Battalion, the army's last all African-American unit, as a gunner and tank driver in the Korean Conflict. He was decorated twice, with a Purple Heart and an Oak Leaf Cluster for taking hits in the trenches. Later, when Stubb was reassigned as a Mess Sergeant, his cooking became so popular that many officers tried to have Stubb transferred to their units, but he refused. In a way, Stubb's mess hall was the first incarnation of a Stubb's barbecue restaurant.

In the Army, Stubb had a duty to feed his men adequately and on time. But Stubb always wanted to do more. He started broadcasting popular records on the field radio so his buddies—

whether they were in tents, trenches, or tanks—could hear them. This feel-good combination of music and food stretched from the brush arbor revivals of Stubb's childhood, to the last days of his life, and not even a war could stop the music for Sergeant C. B. Stubblefield.

Never wasting food or an opportunity to please, Stubb fried onion peelings in the morning, letting the aroma waft through camp to whet appetites (not that anyone needed extra encouragement). Stubb considered each meal a challenge, and he turned the most meager provisions into meals the men would look forward to, including growing Texas tomatoes in Korean soil. One time, he commandeered some Jell-O to make ice cream for the troops, and was known for making chili on the hot tailpipe of an army tank. While the troops enjoyed his cooking, Stubb told stories of growing up in Texas, and somehow home didn't seem quite so far away.

Stubb Befriends the Blues

Fort Hood is a 60-mile drive north of Austin, Texas, and when he was stationed there, Sergeant Stubb headed to Austin as often as he could. Today, Austin is known as "the live music capital of the world," where top acts play country, rock, jazz, and blues, in Austin's lively entertainment district. But in the 1950s, Austin's hottest music was happening in small clubs and juke joints on the black side of town. Muddy Waters, B.B. King, John Lee Hooker, Gatemouth Brown, even Ike and Tina Turner, all played what's known as "the Chitlin' Circuit"—clubs where

African-Americans felt comfortable at a time when segregation still permeated Texas.

Sergeant Stubb made friends with many of these artists, hanging out with them until the sun came up or he was due back at base, whichever came last. Years later, Stubb booked many of the same blues artists to perform in Lubbock, in large rented halls or at the fairgrounds across the street from Stubb's restaurant. When the show was over, the acts headed over to Stubb's restaurant to jam for free. Or at least for a plate full of ribs, once again playing until the sun came up—or in this case, until the brisket and the beer ran dry.

Stubb Starts Smokin'

Stubb was honorably discharged from the Army in 1957 and returned to Lubbock. He enrolled in vocational welding school, on the GI Bill. The skill proved valuable to him later, when he hand-welded his own barbecue pits, but jobs were scarce. Instead, he spent most of a decade working at the town's cottonseed oil mill—it paid the bills, but it wasn't fulfilling.

Stubb had a hankering to make barbecue, and he wanted to make it his way. "I found nowhere did they have the kind of barbecue I could cook," he said. "I guess what was lacking was spirit and love and happiness and smiles. When I smell barbecue, I want to smell something that makes me feel better than I already feel."

Stubb became a self-taught pit master, and to perfect his skills, he sought out West Texas barbecue legend Amos Gamble. But Ol' Man Gamble wouldn't share his secrets, not even with his own family. So Stubb ate at Gamble's place as often as his paycheck allowed, studying Gamble's technique on his own. Over time, Stubb worked out his own methods of smoking meat, to deepen the flavor, and like Amos, he saw the importance of creating a complex, complementary sauce.

As he studied the secrets of great barbecue, Stubb pledged, as much to himself as to anyone in earshot, "I was born hungry, and someday I'm going to feed the world."

Stubb made the first big step toward that goal in 1968. He opened a 75-seat restaurant in a weathered, white stucco building across from the Lubbock fairgrounds, and christened it Stubb's Legendary Bar-B-Que. Inside, he posted a hand-painted sign reading, "There will be no BAD talk or LOUD talk in this PLACE," and in one corner he installed a jukebox, packed with vintage blues.

One afternoon, Stubb picked up a young hitchhiker, whom he would later know as Jesse "Guitar" Taylor, and took him as far down the road as Stubb's Bar-B-Que. Jesse had passed the place many times. The sound of old blues coming from the jukebox got him curious, but as inviting as the barbecue smelled, he never ventured into the ramshackle restaurant.

When Stubb pulled up to the screen door, Jesse said, "Wow! You go into this place?" Stubb proudly replied, "Sir, I own this place." He then told Jesse there was a barbecue sandwich and cold beer waiting inside just for him.

This was the beginning of a great friendship that united live music and Stubb's barbecue. Jesse quickly invited his musician friends to meet him at Stubb's for a Sunday night jam. These jam sessions grew into regular events. They gave birth to a movement that became ground zero for Texas music, and permanently cemented the friendships of Stubb and a stage full of talented Texas musicians.

Legendary Barbecue, Legendary Music

Stubb opened each weekly jam session by inviting the musicians over for Sunday dinner. Joe Ely, Terry Allen, Jimmie Dale Gilmore, Jesse "Guitar" Taylor, and other up-and-comers expected barbecue, but Stubb would feed them a sit-down meal of turkey, dressing, collards, and cornmeal dumplings. After their food settled, they'd pull out their instruments and jam late into the night.

Before long, big-name performers like Willie Nelson, B.B. King, Linda Ronstadt, and George Thorogood dropped by when they were in town—or anywhere near Lubbock. Grammy winner

Tom T. Hall even wrote a song about Stubb's Bar-B-Que—"The Great East Broadway Onion Championship of 1978"—about an early morning pool game between Hall and Ely, where they used an onion instead of a cue ball. Blues guitarist Stevie Ray Vaughan came in regularly, and learned to play Tin Pan Alley by listening to James Reed's version on Stubb's jukebox.

Sometimes Stubb himself would take the microphone to sing solo, or accompany the musicians. People came from all over for the barbecue, the music, and the all-around easygoin' atmosphere that became Stubb's trademark.

Stubb Moves to Austin

In 1985 a series of unfortunate circumstances forced Stubb to close his beloved restaurant. "Let's put it this way, I got run out of Lubbock 'cause I was broke, busted, and disgusted. I can't fight the IRS with barbecue and sauce," he told *Texas Monthly*. To which the magazine added, "That's a shame, because if he could, it would be no contest."

Stubb joined his musician friends in Austin and began selling his barbecue out of Antone's, a blues club near the University of Texas. In 1986, in Austin, he opened his second restaurant, Stubb's Bar-B-Q, where he revived the jam session tradition, featuring many of the same Lubbock musicians, including Joe Ely, Butch Hancock, and the Maines Brothers. Today, Stubb's Bar-B-Q Restaurant serves barbecue, cold beer, and live music at a historic building, handpicked by Stubb himself, in the midst of Austin's entertainment district. (To learn more about the restaurant, visit www.stubbsaustin.com.)

Stubb's Legendary Kitchen

Stubb hand-bottled his first sauce for retail sales in Joe and Sharon Ely's home kitchen. A few weeks later, when Joe appeared on *Late Night with David Letterman*, he gave a few of these bottles to bandleader Paul Schaeffer and Letterman's staff. The buzz about Stubb's sauce spread like wildfire on a windy day. In 1992, Stubb himself appeared on *Late Night with*

David Letterman, cooking barbecue and feeding the entire studio audience. When Letterman asked what Stubb put in his sauce, he simply replied, "Love and happiness."

In May 1996, Stubb died at his home in Austin with his longtime companion, Cindy Jones, at his side. During his life, he always served a free hot meal to anyone who needed it, and he also served a host of celebrities, including President Jimmy Carter, Johnny and June Carter Cash, and the Rolling Stones.

Before Stubb died, he proudly preserved the art of barbecuing "Stubb-style" in a line of products known as Stubb's Legendary Kitchen. "My life is in these bottles," he said, and no truer words were spoken.

Now, with Stubb's Legendary Kitchen and the recipes in this book, home cooks can taste for themselves the life, and all the love and happiness, that aptly earned Stubb the title "West Texas King of Barbecue and the Blues."

Welcome to Stubb's Legendary Kitchen: Love and Happiness to You

Stubb's Legendary Bar-B-Q products are known throughout Texas and the world as the best in barbecue. Born from the hickory pit behind Stubb's restaurant, they're the heart and soul of Stubb's Legendary Kitchen. Here's how to use them in these recipes:

Stubb's Bar-B-Q Sauces

Stubb's Bar-B-Q Sauces are like no other sauces on the market. Most of them share a tangy vinegar kick, in a lively tomato base. If you make these recipes with other barbecue sauces, you may need to adjust the flavorings—other sauces are usually sweeter. Except for Stubb's Smokey Mesquite Barb-B-Q Sauce: It's kissed with molasses and just perfect for recipes that call for a sauce on the sweet side. So take your pick from Stubb's Bar-B-Q Sauce in Original, Mild, Spicy, and Smokey Mesquite varieties.

To get the best out of these Bar-B-Q Sauces, try the three-step system to mastering the art of barbecuing: Start with the Bar-B-Q Rubs before cooking, then baste your barbecue with the

Moppin' Sauce during cooking, and finally, pour warm Bar-B-Q Sauce over the meat when it's ready to be served, or pass it on the side.

Stubb's Bar-B-Q Rubs

Stubb's blends of seasonings perfectly accent the taste of barbecue while helping seal in natural flavors. But they're also good as all-purpose seasonings. Each one adds its own spicy, herbal, citrus, or mustard notes. Try them in this book's recipes instead of traditional seasoning, on poultry, fish, meats, vegetables, and even salads. Stubb's Spice Rub comes in Original Bar-B-Q, Chile-Lime, Rosemary-Ginger, and Herbal Mustard varieties.

Stubb's Moppin' Sauce

Stubb's Moppin' Sauce is a thick, tangy, robust basting sauce used during cooking to keep the meat moist, tender, and flavorful. But it's not just for moppin'—just a small amount sharpens up your favorite marinade, bottled steak sauce, or basting sauce for cooking indoors or out.

Stubb's Marinades

Stubb's blends of herbs and spices are specially crafted to complement all cuts of meat and poultry. Marinate for 30 minutes to 4 hours to go from ordinary to extraordinary. But Stubb's Marinades also jazz up the flavors in a brining solution, or try them instead of the braising liquid in a pot roast. And here's a special tip: A small amount in salad dressings, in place of vinegar, makes the whole dish sparkle with spirit and spice. (They're good replacements for soy sauce and Worcestershire sauce in some recipes, too.) Stubb's Marinades come in three flavors: Pork, Chicken, or Beef; each one has its own unique seasoning power, so feel free to use them interchangeably.

Stubb's Wicked Chicken Wing Sauce

Not just for chicken wings, Stubb's Wing Sauces provide that extra spicy flavoring that brings tearful smiles of joy! Original packs a fiery kick, and Inferno merits a full four-alarm rating. Mix them with fruity glazes or traditional marinades and sauces to ramp up the spice and boost up your barbecue.

Stubb's Liquid Smoke

Indoors or out, Stubb's Liquid Smoke adds natural smoke flavor to the foods you love the most. Take your pick from Hickory or Mesquite, and sprinkle a few drops on meats or vegetables as they cook.

Grilling Jargon and Barbecue Basics

Stubb cooked on a big, black, hand-welded "pit"—a restaurant-size barbecue with a wood-burning compartment. Hardwood acted as his main fuel and as a smoky "flavorizer." But the barbecue recipes in this book are designed with the home cook in mind. You can cook them on any consumer grill, charcoal or gas, with or without smoke, for irresistible, lip-smackin' results.

Temperature and Technique

When it comes to outdoor cooking, how hot is hot? Follow this grilling guide to get the best results from these recipes.

Hand-to-Heat Method: To test the temperature of a grill using the "hand-to-heat" method, hold an open palm 4 to 5 inches above the grill, facing down. Count how long it takes before you pull your hand back. (Relax, you'll instinctively retract your hand before you let it burn.)

> **High heat** = 2 seconds
> **Medium-high heat** = 3 seconds
> **Medium heat** = 4 seconds
> **Low heat** = 6 seconds

Thermometer Method: If your gas grill comes with a thermometer on the lid, close the lid, fire up the gas burners, and use these corresponding temperatures as a guide:

High heat = 450° to 550°F
Medium heat = 350° to 450°F
Low heat = 250° to 350°F

When your grill reaches the desired temperature, place your food on the grate, and grill—directly or indirectly—according to the recipe.

Direct and Indirect Heat

Direct heat means cooking right over the heat source (either hot coals or a gas burner). It's like using an oven broiler, only the heat comes from below, rather than from above. Direct heat cooks foods quickly, gives all foods a golden, mouth-watering exterior, and is used to burn in those classic "grill marks." When recipes call for starting a food over high direct heat, then moving it to medium direct heat (or low direct heat), set up your grill with varying heat zones. That is, create a high-heat area with lots of red-hot coals, and a lower-heat area with fewer, less intense coals. For gas grills, simply adjust the heat by turning the gas-flow knobs.

Indirect heat is used for slower, gentler cooking and to bring the interior temperature of large meats and thick pieces into the acceptable range of being "done." The food rests above an unlit area of the grill, and the heat comes from coals or a gas burner on one or both sides of the food, but never directly below it. Pile the coals in the center and cook foods on the outer grilling area, or push the coals to the outer edges and cook food in the center of the grill. For gas grills, fire up burners on one or more sides of the food, but never right below it.

Smoking Tips

Smoking with wood chunks or chips is optional, but adds an extra layer of flavor. Use hardwood chunks for charcoal grills, or wood chips for either charcoal or gas grills. Choose hickory, mesquite, or oak for strongly flavored meats. Alder is good for seafood, poultry, and some pork recipes. Cherry and other fruit-woods are very mild and subtle.

Plan on burning 2 wood chunks for 1 hour of smoking, and 1 cup of wood chips for an hour or less of smoking. Soak wood chunks in water for 1 hour, and chips for 30 minutes (or follow the manufacturer's directions). Then drain them.

For charcoal grills, distribute the wood chips or chunks directly over the coals. For a gas grill, pour the chips into a metal smoking box. You can also spread the chips in an aluminum foil pan or make a tray out of heavy-duty foil. Set the chip container directly on top of the heat source, under the grate. Close the grill lid to trap the smoke. For longer smoking times, you'll need to replenish the grill with more soaked wood as it burns out.

Capers 'n' Creole Deviled Eggs

Stubb never let a friend leave his house hungry. To make sure they didn't, he always seemed to have a platter of deviled eggs on hand. In Stubb's bold style, tart capers, lemon juice, and a robust mustard (Creole or coarse-grain style) put a bright, shiny sparkle into these wow-the-crowd pleasers. —•🍳 MAKES 12 PIECES

6 large eggs, hard-cooked (see Note)

2 tablespoons mayonnaise

1 heaping tablespoon mustard (Creole or coarse grain)

4 teaspoons freshly squeezed lemon juice

1 tablespoon finely minced scallion (green and white parts)

Salt and freshly ground black pepper to taste

Paprika, for garnish

36 capers, drained, for garnish

1. Shell the eggs, cut them in half lengthwise, and pop the yolks into a mixing bowl. With a fork, mash the yolks with the mayonnaise, mustard, lemon juice, and scallion. Mix in salt and pepper. The mixture should have very pronounced lemon and mustard flavors, so add more if you feel it needs more zing. (Remember: Chilling makes flavors less perceptible, so you may need to add more seasonings.)

2. Fill the cavity in each egg white half with the yolk mixture. Top with a sprinkle of paprika. Place 3 capers on top of each egg half. Chill till ready to serve. For best flavor, let the eggs come to room temperature, or serve just slightly chilled.

NOTE • To make hard-cooked eggs: Place the eggs in a single layer in large pot, fill the pot with enough cold water to cover by 1 inch, and bring just to a boil over medium-high heat. Turn off the heat and let eggs set in the water for 12 minutes. Plunge the eggs into ice cold water. When cool, drain and refrigerate until ready to peel.

If making potato salad: Cover the potatoes and the eggs with water in a deep pot. (Go ahead and add salt to flavor the potatoes; it won't hurt the eggs.) Bring to a boil over medium-high heat. Immediately reduce the heat to a simmer and set the timer for 12 minutes. Scoop out the eggs with a slotted spoon and plunge them into a large bowl of ice water. Continue to cook the potatoes until tender. When the eggs are cool, peel and use as desired.

Double Chile-Avocado Dip

This dip sounds fiery, but it's actually pretty tame (chileheads can fuel the flame with more chipotle). Avocado flesh discolors when exposed to air, but acidic ingredients help preserve the original green color. To keep the freshly cut avocado from turning brown, immediately pour the lime juice over it and mash it together with the lime and sour cream. Then mash in the remaining ingredients. Because avocados vary in size and flavor, be sure to taste the dip and adjust the seasonings before serving.

—⟶ MAKES ABOUT 1¼ CUPS

1 ripe avocado (5 to 6 ounces)
2 tablespoons freshly squeezed lime juice
3 tablespoons sour cream (regular or low-fat)
2 cloves garlic, minced
1 chopped scallion (green and white parts)
1 (4-ounce) can diced roasted green chiles
¼ teaspoon ground cumin
¼ teaspoon ground chipotle chile or cayenne,
    plus more for garnish
⅛ teaspoon salt, or to taste

1. Halve the avocado and scoop the flesh into a bowl, discarding the pit. Pour the lime juice over the flesh, then add the sour cream. With a fork, mash the mixture together until blended (a few small lumps are okay).

2. Dump in the garlic, scallion, green chiles, cumin, chipotle, and salt. Mash the whole thing together to make a mildly chunky dip. Garnish with a sprinkling of chipotle chile. Cover and chill up to several hours before serving with tortilla chips, or serve on a bed of lettuce as a salad.

Pico de Gallo

"Pico de Gallo" translates as "rooster's beak," an odd name of unknown origins (perhaps a reference to the way the coarsely chopped ingredients are small, like chicken feed). Pico de Gallo is the classic complement to fajitas (see page 31), but it's also an all-purpose Tex-Mex salsa for tacos, guacamole, and just plain tortilla chips. Chop the ingredients up to 2 hours in advance, but don't add the lime juice, salt, or vinegar until serving, or the flavors will dilute.

——◦⤜ MAKES ABOUT 1¼ CUPS

2 large Roma tomatoes, chopped
2 scallions (green and white parts), chopped
2 fresh serranos or jalapeños, stemmed, seeded,
  and finely chopped
½ cup loosely-packed, chopped fresh cilantro
Juice of 1 lime
1 teaspoon red wine vinegar, or to taste
Salt, to taste

1. In a bowl, combine the tomatoes, scallions, chiles, and cilantro. If making in advance, cover and refrigerate until ready to use.

2. Stir in the lime juice, vinegar, and salt. Let the mixture sit for about 5 minutes before serving, but no longer than 30 minutes. Taste before serving to correct the seasonings (it should be pleasantly tart with mild heat).

Jezebel Sauce and Appetizer

If you've never tried this sassy spread, don't be alarmed by the ingredients: Jezebel Sauce may sound a little bit country, but it improvises more like a jazz musician. A little sweet, a little spicy, Jezebel Sauce is a Southern tradition, served with cream cheese and crackers. For a sophisticated spin, serve it with soft goat cheese and toasted baguette slices, or smear a little in a quesadilla. Set it out at cocktail hour with cooked little smokies, spicy salami, or grilled smoked sausage. Pair it with smoked meats on a sandwich, or baste it as a glaze on roast duck or Virginia ham.

——◦❯ MAKES ABOUT 2 CUPS

JEZEBEL SAUCE

1 cup pineapple preserves
⅔ cup apple jelly
5 tablespoons Creole mustard or whole-grain
*   brown mustard*
5 tablespoons prepared horseradish

In a small bowl, combine all ingredients; cover and chill. For best results let the flavors meld overnight. Jezebel Sauce will keep refrigerated at least 4 weeks.

JEZEBEL'S APPETIZER • Southerners pour the sauce right over an 8-ounce brick of cream cheese and then smear the mixture on crackers, or you can set out the sauce and cream cheese separately.

——•⇒ WELCOME TO 108 EAST BROADWAY

Behind every great man is a great woman, and Stubb's wife, Cleo, became the unsung hero in his early barbecue business. As their daughter Doris recalls:

"My momma helped Daddy get his restaurant going. My mother did day-work for a banker in Lubbock, a Mr. Moore, who got my father started financially. He also critiqued Daddy's food. 'Add this, don't put that out, change the flavors. . . .' When Daddy first made potato salad, he'd mash the potatoes, and Mr. Moore said that wasn't right. My momma was a real good cook and never mashed the potatoes. So when the restaurant first started, she cooked the potato salad and other dishes at our home. She'd be up peelin' the potatoes, cookin' beans, making huge peach cobblers, for Daddy to take over to the restaurant. I still have these enormous pots she used." (Later, Stubb developed his own special recipes and made everything at the restaurant himself.)

Mr. Moore and other businessmen were some of Stubb's first customers. Lubbock's downtown lacked good barbecue restaurants, and it was only a few blocks from Stubb's place. So it wasn't uncommon to see bankers, lawyers, and well-heeled civic leaders licking their fingers at Stubb's, but only at lunch. Unless you lived in that part of town, which was mainly warehouses and manufacturing plants, you didn't go down there at night.

Texas Tech University provided Stubb a sparse but enthusiastic stream of customers. Professors began bringing their students and families in for lunch. "My dad was a coach at Texas Tech, and he'd drive the cross-country team over to that area of town to run," recalls Lubbock native Chris Oglesby "because there were hills there. Afterwards he'd take them to Stubb's to eat barbecue." Soon, people of all walks of life were finding out what the local musicians, Stubb's nighttime customers, already knew: Stubb's was *the* place to be.

Wicked Jezebel Ribs

The Wicked Jezebel Glaze in this recipe is fruity, tangy, and mildly spicy with a golden hue. It simply combines Jezebel Sauce (see page 6) with wing sauce. Barbecue and specialty stores sell all sorts of wing sauces, but if you don't have any on hand, just replace the wing sauce here with equal parts barbecue sauce and hot sauce. To complement the fruit and horseradish glaze, mix up the Coriander-Mustard Rub below, or to save time, use a premixed rub, one that's lighter on chiles and stronger in mustard and herb flavors, like Stubb's Herbal Mustard Rub.

——◦→》 SERVES 4 TO 6

2 tablespoons all-purpose seasoning salt

1 tablespoon plus 1 teaspoon sugar

1 tablespoon ground coriander

1 tablespoon ground mustard

1 tablespoon yellow mustard seed

1 tablespoon poultry seasoning

2 teaspoons paprika

1 cup Jezebel Sauce (see page 6; make half the recipe)

¼ cup bottled wing sauce, or equal parts barbecue sauce and hot sauce

Two (2- to 3-pound) racks of baby back ribs

1. In a small bowl, combine the seasoning salt, sugar, coriander, ground mustard, mustard seed, poultry seasoning, and paprika. In another bowl, combine the Jezebel Sauce and wing sauce and refrigerate until ready to use.

2. Pull off the thin membrane from the underside of the ribs (Tip: Once you've loosened a corner of the membrane, grab it with a paper towel and pull; the paper towel keeps it from slipping out of your fingers. Removing the membrane makes ribs easier to eat and allows more spice and smoke flavor to penetrate the ribs.) Blot each rack of ribs with a paper towel to dry. Season the ribs on all sides with the spice rub mixture and pat it in with your fingers. Leave the ribs at room temperature for up to 1 hour if you're planning to grill them soon. Or refrigerate them up to overnight, wrapped tightly in plastic wrap; bring them to room temperature before grilling.

3. Prepare a grill for indirect cooking (see page xix). For a charcoal grill, when the coals are ashed over, rake or spread them out in one part of the grill so the food can cook to the side and not directly over the coals. (For a gas grill, fire up the burners on one part of the grill, so the food can cook to the side of the heat but not directly over it.) Cover the grill and bring it to between 250°F and 275°F.

4. Cook the ribs bone side down, over indirect heat, with the grill lid closed, for 1½ to 2 hours, or until the meat just starts to shrink back from the ends of the bones. (Don't overcook; meat should shrink back less than ¼ inch.) To ensure even cooking, set an oven thermometer next to the ribs, also over indirect heat. During the last 30 minutes of cooking, baste the ribs with the sauce mixture every 10 minutes. Set the rib racks on a baking sheet and cover with foil; let them rest for 10 to 20 minutes, then slice and serve.

"When I smell barbecue, I want to smell something that makes me feel better than I already feel."

—C. B. STUBBLEFIELD

Tender Brined Pork Loin Chops

Thick, boneless pork chops take about two hours to brine, and come out bursting with flavor for almost no effort. Brining does two things: It permeates the meat with flavor, and it helps keep the meat moist. For even deeper flavor in this recipe, replace 1 cup of water with 1 cup of a bottled marinade (such as a lemon-pepper or Italian marinade, or Stubb's Pork Marinade).

Besides being economical, a whole boneless pork loin slices into chops in a snap (or buy precut chops). A 4- to 5-pound loin yields 8 to 10 chops, about 1 inch thick.

—●❥ SERVES 6 TO 8

2¾ cups warm water
¼ cup soy sauce
½ cup sugar
¼ cup kosher salt
4 to 5 pounds boneless pork loin chops, about 1½ inches thick
(8 to 10 chops)
2 tablespoons olive oil

1. In a shallow baking dish, combine the water, soy sauce, sugar, and salt, stirring until the sugar and salt dissolve completely. Submerge the pork in the brine (or place in a zipper-top plastic bag and seal), and brine for 2 hours. Drain the brine. (If desired, the drained uncooked chops may be frozen up to 2 months).

2. Prepare a grill for direct cooking (see page xix). For a charcoal grill, when the coals are ashed over, rake or spread them out in the bottom of the grill so the food can cook directly over the coals. (For a gas grill, fire up the burners so the food can cook directly over the heat.)

3. Rinse the chops and pat dry with paper towels. Coat the chops with the olive oil. Grill the chops over direct medium-high heat, 4 to 5 minutes per side. The chops are done when the center is light pink and the internal temperature reaches 145°F. Serve hot.

Lemon-Tarragon Tenderloin on Cranberry-Almond Salad

This dish sounds more French, or at least Californian, than the typical Stubb meal, but he'd be the first to say that "good food is what brings people together." Here, grilled pork tenderloin, flavored with lemon and tarragon, is sliced and arranged on a bed of salad greens, topped with toasted nuts and a cranberry-Dijon dressing. Ooh-la-la! If you have some, 4 teaspoons of Stubb's own Herbal-Mustard Rub can be substituted for half of the lemon-pepper salt. (To cook in a skillet, brown the pork on all sides in a little oil, then add ⅓ cup of broth, wine, or water; cover and braise on medium-low heat about 15 minutes, turning once.)

—◦≫ SERVES 4

2 tablespoons extra-virgin olive oil
1 tablespoon balsamic vinegar
1 tablespoon rice vinegar
2 teaspoons Dijon mustard
2 tablespoons dried, sweetened cranberries, chopped
8 teaspoons lemon-pepper seasoning salt
2 teaspoons dried tarragon, crumbled
2 pork tenderloins (about 2 pounds total)
1 tablespoon olive oil
6 ounces (1 big bowl) cleaned salad greens, such as watercress, spinach, leaf lettuce, or a mix
¼ cup sliced almonds, toasted (see Note)

1. Preferably in a shaker jar, combine the extra-virgin olive oil, balsamic and rice vinegars, mustard, and cranberries and shake or mix well. Let the dressing sit for 15 minutes or longer, for the cranberries to soften and the flavors to blend. Shake or mix thoroughly before using.

2. In a small bowl, mix together the lemon-pepper salt and tarragon and set aside.

3. Cut the tenderloins in half to make 4 short, plump pieces. Rinse and pat dry with paper towels. Rub the pork with the oil. Generously season all sides with the seasoning mixture.

4. Prepare a grill for direct cooking (see page xix). For a charcoal grill, when the coals are ashed over, rake or spread them out in the bottom of the grill so the food can cook directly over the coals. (For a gas grill, fire up the burners so the food can cook directly over the heat.)

5. Grill the pork over direct medium-high heat for 15 to 20 minutes, turning the pieces after browning on each side; in between turning the pieces, cover the grill so the pork cooks internally. The pork is done when the centers are slightly pink and reach an internal temperature of 150°F. Do not overcook, or the pork will be dry.

6. Let the pork rest a few minutes (or up to 1 hour) before slicing. Lightly toss the greens and almonds with just enough dressing to flavor them, but without overpowering. Slice the pork and arrange on top of the greens. If desired, sprinkle a small amount of dressing and almonds over the pork, as garnish, and serve.

NOTE • Toast sliced almonds in a dry skillet over medium heat, stirring often, until golden brown (about 5 minutes). Or microwave on high in a small microwave-safe dish, in 1-minute bursts, stirring in between, about 5 minutes.

See photo on page vi.

Chorizo Joes

C. B. Stubblefield's gift for mixin' up just the right combination of spices and seasonings led him to create Stubb's Original Barbecue Sauce. With a tad more vinegar than most sauces, it's ideal for producing the sweet-tart balance of traditional Sloppy Joes. (If you use a sweeter sauce in this mix, you'll need to round it out with a splash or two of red wine vinegar.)

Mexican chorizo, a spicy raw pork sausage, adds another spicy punch to this dish, and is sold in bulk or in links. If using links, slit the skins, and fry up just the meat. Don't use Spanish-style chorizo; it's cured and hard, and not right for this recipe.

—◦⇒ SERVES 4

1 pound ground chuck (80% lean)
12 ounces Mexican pork chorizo (see Headnote)
1½ cups diced onion (about 1 large)
1 cup barbecue sauce
½ cup water
Salt and freshly ground black pepper, to taste
Red wine vinegar, to taste
4 hamburger buns, toasted

1. In a large skillet over medium-high heat, cook the beef and chorizo together, breaking up the meat with a wooden spoon. When the meats are crumbled, push them to one side of the pan, tilt the pan to collect the oil, then spoon off and discard the oil.
2. Stir the onion into the meats and cook, stirring, until the onion softens, about 3 minutes. Stir in the barbecue sauce and water, reduce the heat, and simmer, stirring occasionally, for 15 to 20 minutes; the mixture is done when it's moist and glazed, neither dry nor soupy. Taste, and add salt, pepper, or vinegar as needed. (The mixture may be made 2 days in advance and re-frigerated; reheat before using.) Serve hot, in toasted hamburger buns, with plenty of napkins.

"Short-Cut" Pulled Pork

On the barbecue circuit, when whole pork shoulders cook for a full day, low and slow, they become succulent, savory creatures. But not everyone has the time or the appetite to accommodate a 16-pound steamin' hunk of meat. However, if you carve a more manageable 4-pound pork shoulder or butt into big chunks—or better yet, buy the meat precut into "country style ribs"—you're just a few hours away from eatin' high on the hog. Well-marbled chunks or strips, set in a disposable foil pan, cook in under three hours. (For indoor cooking, toss the pork chunks into a crock-pot, turn the power to low, and walk away for about five hours. The chunks will be browned outside, and meltingly tender.)

Once cooked, the pork takes on multiple personalities. For Pulled Pork, shred or finely chop the pork into bits. Heat it with a cup of Stubb's Pork Marinade for a spicy Texas twang, or mix it with ¼ cup cider vinegar and ¾ cup barbecue sauce for a North Carolina accent. And for Tex-Mex "carnitas" filling, chop the pork into little bits and serve with Pico de Gallo (see page 5), wrapped in warm tortillas.

—⟶⟫ SERVES 4 TO 6

2 tablespoons barbecue seasoning or rub
2 tablespoons granulated garlic or garlic powder
2 teaspoons black pepper
About 1½ teaspoons salt (see Note)
4 pounds pork butt, or "country-style" ribs
3 cups wood chips, or 4 to 5 chunks, soaked (optional)

1. In a small bowl, combine the barbecue seasoning, garlic, pepper, and salt. If using pork butt, chop it into thick strips or chunks, about the size of a small fist. Place the pork in a large disposable aluminum foil pan. Coat the pork on all sides with the spice rub.

2. Prepare a grill for indirect cooking (see page xix). For a charcoal grill, when the coals are ashed over, rake or spread them out in one part of the grill so the food can cook to the side and not directly over the coals. (For a gas grill, fire up the burners on one part of the grill, so the food can cook to the side of the heat but not directly over it.) Cover the grill and bring it to around 250°F. Drain and add half of the wood (if using) for smoking.

3. Set the pan of pork over indirect heat and cook in the covered grill for about 3 hours. To ensure even cooking, set an oven thermometer next to the pan, also over indirect heat. Every hour, check it and add more fuel and wood as needed to maintain a smoky 250°F heat. The pork is done when the pieces are browned on the outside but tender on the inside. When the meat reaches an internal temperature of 165°F to 175°F, it's cooked enough to be sliced. If it's well marbled with fat, you can cook it to 190°F, suitable for shredding.

NOTE • Barbecue seasonings and rubs contain varying amounts of salt. The finished mix for this recipe should be balanced with a pronounced salt flavor, but if it tastes too salty then it probably is. Add salt to the other seasonings sparingly at first, taste, and adjust the proportions accordingly.

Beef, Bold and Beautiful

STUBB'S TIPS FOR A PERFECT BRISKET

Stubb was famous for all kinds of barbecue, but his briskets brought tears of joy and admiration to even the burliest Texans. Stubb's brisket rolls across the tongue in a delectable sequence: the salty-spicy outer crust, the quarter-inch smoke ring, and the delicious bite of fork-tender meat. That's the beauty of a Stubb's brisket, and these are his tips for cooking brisket at home.

Preparing a Whole Brisket

Briskets are only available in select or choice grades, and most come in 8- to 12-pound shrink-wrapped plastic "packer" cases. Briskets are sometimes sold halved as a thick and fatty *point* cut, and a thinner, leaner *flat* cut. Traditional pit barbecuers tackle only the whole brisket, but the accompanying recipe has instructions for half a brisket.

If you buy a whole brisket, prepare yourself: a regular-size cutting board is no match for these monsters. If you don't have an extra large board, lay out 3 to 4 feet of butcher or parchment paper as a prep board. Most "packer" briskets come untrimmed. The fat helps the cooking process, but you don't want more than a quarter- to half-inch of fat anywhere on the outer surface of the brisket. So rinse the brisket and pat it dry with paper towels, then give it a trim.

The Rub

Stubb always had his rub ready to go, then generously poured it onto the brisket, flipping the brisket and firmly patting the spice mix over every inch. Some folks then refrigerate briskets overnight, but Stubb went straight to the grill.

After patting the rub generously onto the brisket, he mopped the brisket with his mopping sauce, and then sprinkled more rub on over the sauce before placing the brisket in his pit. Mopping sauces are a matter of taste; some cooks don't use a mopping sauce at all. The choice is yours (see more about mops below).

Smoking

Briskets can cook on any type of "pit," including charcoal and gas grills and dedicated smokers, as long as they have a lid and a way to control the temperature. A low heat, over many hours, breaks down the tough connective tissue and renders the fat, melting it down, inside and outside the brisket. The process tenderizes the meat, and the rich smoke flavor penetrates deep into the brisket.

Stubb cooked his briskets at 210°F to 235°F. Variances in temperature will change your levels of success, but if you shoot for 225°F you'll be fine. The 275°F to 300°F range reduces cooking time, but also significantly reduces the tenderness and smokiness of the meat. Built-in thermometers, positioned on a grill lid, aren't accurate enough for briskets. Instead, rely on an oven thermometer set inside the grill, near the meat. If your grill lid has an opening to peek through, face the thermometer gauge so you can monitor it without lifting the lid.

The Wood

Pick your favorite as long as it's a hardwood (softwood burns too quickly).

Stubb preferred post oak. "You gotta use what the Lord gives you. . . . If you live in Tennessee, you use hickory; if you live in central Texas, you use post oak," he'd say. When oak was scarce, he used pecan or mesquite, or a mix of woods.

Stubb's Moppin' Sauce and Technique

After applying the first mop on top of the rub, Stubb mopped his briskets every two to three hours with a mopping sauce. Mopping sauces usually consist of vinegar (white or cider) and oil, with pepper, salt, and other spices (he bottled his own recipe, which has a tart, mustard-kissed kick, as Stubb's Moppin' Sauce). He said a good mop keeps the meat moist and seals it, and the acidity helps tenderize it. Stubb always smoked brisket with the fat side up, never flipping it. He'd lift it gently, now and then, to mop or move it relative to the heat, but he'd never "rough up" the brisket, which ruins the tasty rub 'n' mop crust. Stubb always stopped using the moppin' sauce an hour or longer before the brisket was ready, to allow the vinegar in the mop to evaporate.

Finishing and Slicing Brisket

The brisket is done when a meat thermometer registers an internal temperature of 185°F, taken in the larger half of the brisket, in the meaty (not fatty) area. Brisket needs to rest before slicing, at least 15 minutes, and preferably 45 minutes, tented with foil, so the meat can reabsorb the juices.

Briskets aren't at all like other roasts, so to slice a brisket properly, you need to understand the cut's internal structure: A ribbon of fat runs horizontally through the meat, from the thick end to the thin end. It separates what's known as the top "fat cap" from the "lean flat" of the bottom. Slice along it, and scrape away the fat separating the two halves from each other. Next, slice the meaty halves of the brisket against, or across, the grain. Serve thin slices of each on the same plate; one is nicely marbled and fat-flavored inside, and the other is drier and leaner. Together, they balance out to make the perfect bite of brisket.

Smoked Whole (or Half) Brisket

Smoking a whole beef brisket requires deep commitment—literally. Plan on 1½ hours per pound of brisket. This means at least 15 hours for a "small" 10-pound brisket, and 24 hours for a 16-pounder! But once the meat's on the grill, the hard labor's done. Just tend to the temperature, the smoke, and, if desired, give it an occasional mop.

⟶•⟫ (ALLOW 1 POUND OF UNCOOKED BRISKET PER COOKED SERVING PORTION)

Half-Brisket Short Cut

If the prospect of tending your 'cue all day and into the night overwhelms, then cook half of a brisket, trimmed to the 4- to 5-pound range. The two halves of a brisket are the *point* and the *flat* cuts, with the point cut being fattier but more tender on the grill. Follow the basic instructions below, but when the meat's internal temperature reaches 160°F, after about 4 hours on the grill, seal the meat tightly in heavy-duty aluminum foil. Finish cooking on the grill (without smoke) or on a pan in a 225°F oven, until the internal temperature reaches 185°F, about 2 more hours. With this method, you can cook one or both halves simultaneously, in about 6 hours total cooking time, spending the last few hours indoors if you like, or if the weather works against you.

STUBB'S RESTAURANT RUB FOR MEATS
Makes about 1½ cups; enough for a large brisket or 3 slabs of ribs

½ cup black pepper, preferably medium ground
½ cup Stubb's Bar-B-Q Spice Rub
¼ cup granulated garlic or garlic powder
3 tablespoons onion powder
2 tablespoons all-purpose seasoning salt

One 9- to 11-pound trimmed brisket, with about a ¼-inch
   layer of fat
2 cups Stubb's Moppin' Sauce (optional)
8 cups wood chips, or 12 chunks, soaked
Barbecue sauce (optional)

1. In a small bowl, combine the pepper, Spice Rub, granulated garlic, onion powder, and seasoning salt and set aside.
2. Rinse the brisket and pat dry with paper towels. Generously coat the brisket with the spice rub mixture on all sides. Brush with mopping sauce (if using). Let it come to room temperature while the grill fires up.
3. Prepare a grill for indirect cooking (see page xix). For a charcoal grill, when the coals are ashed over, rake or spread them out in one part of the grill so the food can cook to the side and not directly over the coals. (For a gas grill, fire up the burners on one part of the grill, so the food can cook to the side of the heat but not directly over it.) Cover the grill and bring it to around 225°F. Drain and add one-quarter of the wood for smoking.
4. Set the brisket over indirect heat and cook about 1½ hours per pound. To ensure even cooking, set an oven thermometer next to the brisket, also over indirect heat. Every hour, check it and add more fuel and wood as needed to maintain a smoky 225°F heat. Cook, mopping every 2 to 3 hours (stop moppin' one to two hours before you think the brisket will be done), until the internal temperature reaches 185°F. Let the brisket rest 15 to 45 minutes. Slice the meat against the grain and serve plain or with barbecue sauce on the side.

Marley 'Cue Meatloaf

If C. B. Stubblefield and Bob Marley ever got the chance to jam on stage, they'd have made bluesy reggae music together. And if they jammed in the kitchen, this is the meatloaf they'd come up with. A touch of Jamaican allspice, dried tropical fruit, and blasts of barbecue seasoning and sauce make for a mellow meatloaf, mon.

Packages of mixed dried fruit bits come in different varieties, and specialty stores often sell them in bulk. If you can't find the tropical blend (with mangoes, coconut, and papaya), use any variety of dried fruit. Instead of grilling, you may also bake this meatloaf in a greased baking dish at 350°F for about 1 hour and 15 minutes.

—●⫸ SERVES 4

1 cup dried fruit bits, preferably tropical blend
½ cup apple juice
1 pound breakfast sausage
1 pound ground beef (ground round or chuck)
1 cup fresh bread crumbs
½ cup finely chopped onion
3 tablespoons whipping cream
2 large eggs
2 teaspoons barbecue seasoning or rub
1 teaspoon ground allspice
¼ cup barbecue sauce
¼ cup ketchup

1. In a large bowl, combine the fruit bits with the apple juice and let soak for 10 minutes.

2. Add the sausage, beef, bread crumbs, onion, cream, eggs, seasoning, and allspice. With clean hands, mix everything together. In a lightly greased foil pan (about 9 x 12 inches), shape the meat into a 9 x 5-inch loaf.

3. In a small bowl, combine the barbecue sauce and ketchup to use as the topping and set aside.

4. Prepare a grill for indirect cooking (see page xix, or see Headnote for oven baking). For a charcoal grill, when the coals are ashed over, rake or spread them out in one part of the grill so the food can cook to the side and not directly over the coals. (For a gas grill, fire up the burners on one part of the grill, so the food can cook to the side of the heat but not directly over it.) Cover the grill and bring it to medium temperature (350°F to 400°F).

5. Cook the meatloaf in its pan over indirect heat, in a covered grill, for 1 to 1½ hours, smearing the loaf with the topping about halfway through. The meatloaf is done when the internal temperature measures 155°F. Let it rest for 10 minutes, then slice and serve.

When asked how he was while in the hospital: "My spark plugs ain't firing, and I got this tornado loose in my chest."

—C. B. STUBBLEFIELD

Smokey Tex-Mex Fajitas

Folks may wonder where the cast-iron plate with sizzling bell peppers, tomatoes, and guacamole are in this recipe. Look for them at popular restaurant chains, but not in authentic Tex-Mex presentations. Real fajitas come with two things only: tortillas and Pico de Gallo. And when the fajitas are good, that's all you need.

—•» SERVES 4

2 pounds beef skirt steak
1½ teaspoons ground cumin
1 teaspoon granulated garlic or garlic powder
3 tablespoons freshly squeezed lime juice
1 tablespoon jalapeño pickling liquid
2 tablespoons olive oil
½ onion, sliced thin
¼ cup sliced pickled jalapeños ("en escabeche")
Pico de Gallo (see page 5)
1 tablespoon soy sauce
1 tablespoon liquid smoke (optional)
Warm flour tortillas

1. Lay out the skirt steak in a dish for marinating (oblong baking dishes work great). (After seasoning, you can fold the steak, overlapping it onto itself, if it's too long to fit in the dish.)

2. Sprinkle the cumin and garlic over all sides of the steak. Pour the lime juice, jalapeño liquid, and olive oil over the steak, and slosh the steak around to coat all sides. Place the onion and jalapeños under the steak, on top of it, and between any ends that were folded over. Cover and refrigerate. Marinate for at least 4 hours, preferably overnight. Turn the steak around in the dish once during marinating.

3. About 30 minutes before eating, prepare the Pico de Gallo and refrigerate.

4. Prepare a grill for direct cooking (see page xix). For a charcoal grill, when the coals are ashed over, rake or spread them out in the bottom of the grill so the food can cook directly over the coals. (For a gas grill, fire up the burners so the food can cook directly over the heat.)

5. Just before grilling, pour the soy sauce over the meat, to help it brown. Grill over direct high heat. As the meat cooks, sprinkle on the liquid smoke (if using), first on one side, then on the other. When the steak has good grill marks on one side, flip it over and cook until the interior is done, 6 to 8 minutes total cooking time on a really hot grill, or up to 10 minutes on a less efficient grill. Fajitas are best when cooked medium rare, slightly pink, and really juicy on the inside.

6. Let the steak rest 5 minutes before slicing. To serve, slice the steak into thin strips. Load a warmed flour tortilla with the steak, and spoon some Pico de Gallo on top. Tex-Mex heaven! (While the meat rests, you can boil the remaining marinade and onions at least 1 minute. Pour over the sliced steak before serving.)

THERE WILL BE NO BAD TALK, OR LOUD TALK IN THIS PLACE.

Korean Steak, Stubb-Style

When Stubb served in Korea, he discovered that Koreans and Texans have much in common: Both love beef, chili peppers and grilling over a charcoal pit. This Korean marinade may also be used to grill thin slices of beef (known as bulgogi), rather than a whole steak. (To put a touch of Texas in this dish, replace half the soy sauce with Stubb's Beef Marinade.) It's also dynamite on lamb, particularly when charcoal grilled. Serve with steamed rice and a cucumber salad, tossed with a sesame dressing.

—⊶❯❯ SERVES 4

2 pounds beef flank steak or sirloin
4 scallions (green and white parts)
⅓ cup packed brown sugar
¼ cup soy sauce
2 tablespoons minced garlic
2 tablespoons minced fresh ginger
4 teaspoons sesame oil
2 tablespoons sesame seeds, toasted (see Note)
¼ teaspoon crushed red pepper flakes (optional)
1 tablespoon dry sherry

1. Score the beef on each side with intersecting cuts ¾ inch apart to create a diamond pattern; cut only lightly into the meat, about ⅛ inch deep. Slice the scallions diagonally into ¾-inch lengths.

2. In a baking dish or shallow pan, combine the brown sugar, soy sauce, garlic, ginger, sesame oil and seeds, pepper flakes, and sherry. Stir in the scallions, then add the beef, coating well with the marinade. Cover and marinate, refrigerated, preferably for 8 hours (or from 1 hour to overnight), turning the beef once or twice.

3. Prepare a grill for direct cooking (see page xix). For a charcoal grill, when the coals are ashed over, rake or spread them out in the bottom of the grill so the food can cook directly over the coals. (For a gas grill, fire up the burners so the food can cook directly over the heat.)

4. Grill the steak over direct high heat, flipping once, long enough to lightly char the scored edges of the meat, making them crisp and crunchy, without overcooking the interior. (Allow 8 to 10 minutes total for medium-rare.)

5. Let the steak rest for 10 minutes. If desired, boil the marinade for 1 full minute or more, to use as a sauce. Slice the steak against the grain into thin strips and serve drizzled with the cooked marinade.

NOTE • Toast sesame seeds in a dry skillet over medium heat, stirring often, until golden brown and aromatic, 3 to 5 minutes. Or buy the seeds already toasted.

> **"Blues relates to a real feelin'. And that's where I want my barbecue to come from: real feelin'."**
>
> **—C. B. STUBBLEFIELD**

Toasted Pecan Burgers

Crunchy pecans, sweet red onion, and barbecue sauce—now
that's what makes a burger better!

—◦≫ MAKES 3 LARGE (PREFERABLE) OR 4 AVERAGE-SIZE BURGERS

1 pound ground chuck
¼ cup chopped red onion
¼ cup chopped pecans, toasted (see Note)
1 tablespoon finely chopped green bell pepper
3 tablespoons barbecue sauce
2 tablespoons barbecue seasoning or rub
Lettuce, mayonnaise, and toasted buns, for serving

1. Mix together the chuck, onion, pecans, bell pepper, sauce,
and seasoning. Shape into 3 large or 4 average-size patties. (The
burgers may be mixed and shaped earlier in the day; refrigerate
until ready to use.)
2. Prepare a grill for direct cooking (see page xix). For a charcoal grill, when the coals are ashed over, rake or spread them out
in the bottom of the grill so the food can cook directly over the
coals. (For a gas grill, fire up the burners so the food can cook
directly over the heat.)
3. Grill the burgers over direct medium heat, first on one side
then on the other, 7 to 10 minutes, until they reach your desired
degree of doneness. (Medium burgers register an internal temperature of 160°F.) Serve with lettuce, mayonnaise, and toasted
buns.

NOTE · Heat the chopped pecans in a skillet over low heat, stirring often until they start to brown on the edges. The oil in nuts
continues to cook after the heat is turned off, so don't overcook
them or they'll taste bitter.

Stubb's Slow Cooked Rosemary-Garlic Pot Roast

Some barbecue marinades and seasonings work as well indoors as they do outdoors. Here, a rosemary-based rub and a beefy marinade jump into the crock-pot for a hearty, cold-weather meal. Some markets sell their own chunky blend of pot roast vegetables, but it's easy enough to make your own—just cut a couple stalks of celery into 1-inch pieces; chunk up an equal amount of carrots or use two big handfuls of baby carrots; chop an onion into large chunks; and throw in 5 or 6 small red potatoes. Toss everything into a slow cooker (also known as a crock-pot) for a few hours, and dinner is done.

—⊶❯❯ SERVES 4

2 to 3 pounds mixed pot roast vegetables (see Headnote)
5 whole cloves garlic
One 3-pound boneless beef chuck roast
3 tablespoons Stubb's Rosemary-Ginger Rub
½ cup Stubb's Beef Marinade, (or equal parts soy sauce
    and water)
¼ cup soy sauce
2 sprigs fresh rosemary (optional)
¼ cup water

1. Set the vegetables in the bottom of a medium to large slow cooker, with the potatoes on the top layer. Smash the garlic with the flat of a large knife against a cutting board, and discard the peel. Sprinkle the smashed garlic over the vegetables.

2. Coat the roast with the rub. Set the roast on top of the vegetables, and pour any excess rub over the roast.

3. Pour the marinade and soy sauce over the roast. Enclose the rosemary sprigs (if using) in cheesecloth and drop into the pot. Pour the water around the edges of the pot (not over the roast).

4. Cover and turn the heat to low. Cook 7 to 8 hours, or until the vegetables and meat are tender. Remove the rosemary sprigs and degrease if needed. Serve in shallow bowls, with a bit of meat, vegetables, and broth (and bread for sopping up the juices).

Chili Con Carne

The main thing to remember about chili con carne is that it's a stew. It can be thick and chunky, or juicy with lots of "gravy." Like all good stews, it needs to cook slowly. You can eat the chili right away, but if you let it rest for a few hours, the flavors soften and mingle, and that's when stew develops character. Whether you call them chiles, chilies, chillis, or chilis, these spicy little pods come in hundreds of varieties. Chiles can be fruity and sweet, or hot 'n' mean. There's no single best combination or type of chile, so pick the formula that works for you. Ground chuck (80 percent lean) and ground round (85 percent lean) make a balanced meat mix, but any ground beef that's not too lean works just fine. A course grind gives more texture, and some dedicated chili cooks use only chunks instead of ground meat.

—◦≫ SERVES 4

2 teaspoons olive oil

2 pounds ground beef

1 large onion, diced

6 cloves garlic, chopped

3 tablespoons ground red chile (preferably equal parts pasilla
    or ancho, New Mexico, and chipotle chiles)

2 tablespoons paprika

2 tablespoons ground cumin

2 teaspoons dried oregano, crushed

2 teaspoons sugar

1 teaspoon salt

1 (8-ounce) can tomato sauce

1 cup water

2 teaspoons soy sauce

1. In a heavy pot, heat the oil, then cook the beef over high heat, breaking it up as it cooks, until crumbly.

Chile Con Carne *(continued)*

2. Reduce the heat to medium and stir in the onion and garlic. Cook, stirring, until the onion turns translucent, about 5 minutes, then stir in the chile, paprika, cumin, oregano, sugar, salt, tomato sauce, water, and soy sauce. Bring to a boil, then reduce the heat to low. Cover and simmer, stirring occasionally, for 30 minutes. Cook for another 30 minutes, partially covered. If the chili is too thin for your liking, raise the heat and cook uncovered until it thickens.

3. Serve hot. For best results, let it rest a few hours or overnight, refrigerated, then reheat. Serve with chopped onion, cheese, corn chips, or the condiments of your choice.

Poultry, Pure and Simple

Wicked Chimichurri Wings

Here, the West Texas cowboy goes gaucho. In Argentina, Land of the Gauchos, mounds of spit-roasted meats team up with bowls of "chimichurri sauce." As a marinade, chimichurri sauce infuses foods with a tart (but not hot) parsley-garlic-vinegar blast. Ramp up the flavors with a touch of bottled wing sauce and a hot grill, and you've got a platter of robust, "gotta-eat-more" wings. Try it here, then create your own "Wicked Chimichurri" ribs, steaks, and chops.

The now-famous finger food, Buffalo Chicken Wings, hatched a whole flock of bottled wing sauces. We prefer Stubb's Wicked Wing Sauce for this recipe, but if you don't have any wing sauces on hand, substitute equal parts of bottled hot sauce (the bright red stuff) and barbecue sauce. The flavor won't be quite the same, but it will still be fiery, festive, and finger-lickin' good.

—◦≫ SERVES 4 TO 6

½ cup bottled wing sauce (see Headnote)
¼ cup olive oil
2 tablespoons soy sauce
4 teaspoons red wine vinegar
1 cup tightly packed fresh parsley
4 cloves garlic
2 teaspoons dried oregano
3 to 4 pounds chicken wings

1. Combine the wing sauce, olive oil, soy sauce, vinegar, parsley, garlic, and oregano in the bowl of a food processor. Pulse until pureed and the mixture forms a thick sauce.

2. Fold and tuck the wing tips back behind the drummette, creating a triangle. Marinate the chicken for at least 2 hours, or up to overnight, refrigerated.

3. Prepare a grill for direct cooking (see page xix). For a charcoal grill, when the coals are ashed over, rake or spread them out in the bottom of the grill so the food can cook directly over the coals. (For a gas grill, fire up the burners so the food can cook directly over the heat.)

4. Grill the wings over direct medium heat, until the wings are brown on the outside and the meat is opaque, about 20 minutes total cooking time, flipping them over once or twice during cooking. Serve warm or at room temperature.

Thai Coconut Chicken

Stubb's version of a Thai marinade delivers a true Southeast Asian flavor balance: hot, sour, salty, and sweet. Thighs are the chicken pieces of choice, because they're rich in flavor and don't dry out easily, but other chicken pieces can be substituted. (You can even chop up the meat for stir-frying.) Unsweetened coconut milk, found in the Asian foods aisle, separates; stir the thick cream from the top of the can into the milky liquid before measuring. And if you've got some on hand, swap out Stubb's Pork Marinade for ¼ cup of the soy sauce, to give the dish a zestier kick.

—◦⇒ SERVES 4

STUBB'S THAI COCONUT MARINADE
Makes 1½ cups (enough for 3 pounds of meat)

1½-inch piece of fresh ginger (peeled if woody)
1 scallion (green and white parts)
1 lemon, rinsed and dried
3 cloves garlic
1 cup packed fresh cilantro (about ½ bunch)
¾ cup canned unsweetened coconut milk
¼ cup plus 1 tablespoon soy sauce
¼ cup plus 1 tablespoon (packed) dark brown sugar
½ teaspoon salt

About 3 pounds boneless, skinless chicken thighs

1. Quarter the ginger into chunks for processing. Cut the scallion into 1-inch lengths. With a vegetable peeler, strip off the lemon zest (just the yellow part, not the bitter white pith). Halve the lemon and squeeze out 2 tablespoons of juice.
2. Combine the ginger, scallion, lemon zest, and garlic in the bowl of a food processor and chop finely. Add the lemon juice, cilantro, coconut milk, soy sauce, brown sugar, and salt. Whiz

Thai Coconut Chicken (*continued*)

until everything is finely chopped, scraping down the sides of the container as necessary.

3. Pour the mixture into a container for marinating (a zipper-top plastic bag works great). Add the chicken and coat well with the marinade. Cover and refrigerate at least 2 hours, preferably overnight.

4. Prepare a grill for direct cooking (see page xix). For a charcoal grill, when the coals are ashed over, rake or spread them out in the bottom of the grill so the food can cook directly over the coals. (For a gas grill, fire up the burners so the food can cook directly over the heat.)

5. Drain off the excess marinade from the chicken. Grill the chicken on both sides over direct medium-high heat, flipping halfway through, until the meat is firm and opaque in the center, 10 to 15 minutes total cooking time.

"Music always lives in the heart."

—C. B. STUBBLEFIELD

Grilled Boneless Breasts with Raspberry-Balsamic Glaze

Fruity, tangy, and mildly spicy, the Raspberry-Balsamic Barbecue Sauce turns the humble chicken breast into upscale fare. Besides chicken, brush it on as a finishing sauce or glaze on pork and salmon. For best results, use a traditionally sweet style of barbecue sauce for this recipe (like Stubb's Smokey Mesquite Bar-B-Q Sauce).

For an eye-catching presentation, score the boneless breasts before cooking (described below). Scoring also helps the sauce penetrate more deeply, and the meat cooks more evenly when scored.

—→❖ SERVES 4

½ cup frozen raspberries
¼ cup barbecue sauce (sweet-style)
2 tablespoons honey
4 teaspoons balsamic vinegar
4 (about 1½ pounds) boneless, skinless chicken breasts
About 2 tablespoons olive oil
Salt and freshly ground black pepper

1. Chop the raspberries in a food processor, leaving some texture and small chunks. (Frozen berries chop best, without turning to mush, but thawed berries work fine too.) Add the barbecue sauce, honey, and vinegar and pulse just until combined. When the berries are fully thawed, taste and, if necessary, add more honey or vinegar to balance the sweetness and tartness of the sauce. Set aside half the sauce for passing on the side, and use the remainder on the chicken as it cooks.

2. Prepare a grill for direct cooking (see page xix). For a charcoal grill, when the coals are ashed over, rake or spread them out in the bottom of the grill so the food can cook directly over the

coals. (For a gas grill, fire up the burners so the food can cook directly over the heat.)

3. Score the chicken breasts by making parallel cuts from ⅛ to ¼ inch deep, spaced about ¾ inch apart. Create a diamond pattern by making another set of parallel scores at angles to the first set; make deeper scores in the thicker parts, and shallower scores in the thinner parts. Score the other side of the chicken breasts. Place the breasts in a baking dish or on a large plate. Coat them with the oil. Season both sides with salt and a good dose of pepper.

4. Grill over direct medium-high heat, cooking just long enough to create good grill marks on the first side. Flip the breasts over. While the underside of the breasts cook, spoon the sauce over the cooked side, letting it sink into the scored areas. The total cooking time will be 8 to 10 minutes. Serve hot, passing additional sauce on the side.

"I was born hungry; I want to feed the world."

—C. B. STUBBLEFIELD

Cider-Brined Turkey Breast

Unless you own a walk-in refrigerator, or one with lots of empty shelf space, a whole turkey is tough to brine overnight and still keep cold. But a whole turkey *breast* can fit into a large pot or mixing bowl, brine and all, and still leave room in the fridge for side dishes and dessert. Grilling takes only about 1½ hours, with no basting, and the result is tender, moist meat, slightly sweet with a touch of smoke.

For an even tastier brine, replace 3 cups of the apple cider with two (12-ounce) bottles of prepared marinade. Citrus and acidic based marinades work best in this brine, like lemon-pepper marinade, lime-mesquite marinade, Caribbean jerk marinade, or Stubb's Chicken Marinade.

—➤ SERVES 6 TO 8

¾ cup kosher salt
3 cups warm water
7 cups apple cider
1 cup molasses
1 (5- to 7-pound) whole turkey breast
2 or 3 tablespoons olive oil
1 cup wood chips, or 2 chunks, soaked (optional)

1. In a stockpot or large container, stir the salt and water together until the salt dissolves. Stir in the cider and molasses. Submerge the turkey breast in the brine and refrigerate for 12 to 24 hours; turn the turkey over every few hours if the brine doesn't cover it completely. (If the container won't fit in the fridge, place it in an ice chest and chill well with ice or ice packs, at a maximum temperature of 40°F.)

2. Rinse the turkey breast and pat dry. Rub it all over with the oil and let it come to room temperature about 20 minutes before cooking.

3. Prepare a grill for indirect cooking (see page xix). For a charcoal grill, when the coals are ashed over, rake or spread them out in one part of the grill so the food can cook to the side and not directly over the coals. (For a gas grill, fire up the burners on one part of the grill, so the food can cook to the side of the heat but not directly over it.) Start the wood smoking. Cover the grill and bring it to medium heat, about 350°F.

4. Set the turkey breast skin side up over indirect heat and cook in a closed grill for about 1½ hours. To ensure even cooking, set an oven thermometer next to the brisket, also over indirect heat. If the heat is coming from one side only, rotate the turkey midway through (but leave it skin-side up). Add more fuel and wood as needed to maintain a smoky 350°F heat. The meat is done when it reaches 165°F on a meat thermometer. Let the breast rest 10 minutes before carving.

"You enjoy what you're doing. I love to make people enjoy food."

—C. B. STUBBLEFIELD

Marinated Mustard-Mop Chicken

Tart and tangy, with a mustard and herb kick. The marinade doubles as a mop, for slathering on ribs and other grilled meats. If the weather's bad, you can also broil the chicken, or bake it in a 350°F oven for 30 to 35 minutes.

—◦✈ SERVES 4

⅓ cup cider vinegar
⅓ cup apple juice
5 tablespoons Creole mustard or whole-grain mustard
3 tablespoons Worcestershire sauce
1 teaspoon Italian seasoning, crumbled
1 teaspoon fennel seed, lightly crushed (optional)
½ teaspoon granulated garlic or garlic powder
4 bone-in chicken breasts (3 to 4 pounds total)

1. In a small bowl, combine the vinegar, apple juice, mustard, Worcestershire, Italian seasoning, fennel seed, and garlic powder. Set aside ⅓ cup of the mixture for basting. In a large container, coat the chicken thoroughly with the remaining marinade (a zipper-top plastic bag works great). Marinate the chicken, covered, for at least 2 hours, or up to overnight, refrigerated, moving the pieces around in the marinade from time to time.

2. Prepare a grill for both direct and indirect cooking (see page xix). For a charcoal grill, when the coals are ashed over, rake or spread them out in the bottom of the grill so the food can cook directly over the coals, but leave half the grilling area free of coals. (For a gas grill, fire up the burners so the food can cook directly over the heat, but leave half the grilling area unlit.)

3. Grill the chicken, skin side-down, over direct medium heat, until the skin is crisp and golden, 8 to 10 minutes. Move the pieces around as they cook to prevent charring. Flip the pieces over, move them to indirect heat, and baste with the reserved marinade. Cover the grill and cook, basting occasionally with the marinade-mop, until the juices run clear and the meat is no longer pink, 10 to 15 minutes more.

Rubmaster's Grill-Roasted Drums

The key to a good rub is balance. This one is mildly spicy, slightly herby, and full of flavor without being overpowering. This is the same rub Stubb's Restaurant in Austin uses on their poultry and seafood.

—◦≫ SERVES 4

STUBB'S RESTAURANT POULTRY RUB
(makes about ⅓ cup)

3 tablespoons paprika
2 teaspoons granulated garlic
½ teaspoon cayenne
1½ teaspoons salt
½ teaspoon white pepper
½ teaspoon freshly ground black pepper
½ teaspoon dried thyme
½ teaspoon dried oregano

3½ to 4 pounds chicken drumsticks (12 to 14 pieces)

1. To make the rub, in a small bowl, combine the paprika, granulated garlic, cayenne, salt, white pepper, black pepper, thyme, and oregano.

2. Rinse the drumsticks and pat them dry with paper towels. Arrange the drumsticks on a baking sheet. Generously coat the drumsticks on all sides with the rub, patting it in with your fingertips. Let rest for 1 hour.

3. Prepare a grill for both direct and indirect cooking (see page xix). For a charcoal grill, when the coals are ashed over, rake or spread them out in the bottom of the grill so the food can cook directly over the coals, but leave half the grilling area free of coals. (For a gas grill, fire up the burners so the food can cook directly over the heat, but leave half the grilling area unlit.)

4. Cook the drumsticks over direct medium-high heat until grill marks appear, about 2 minutes per side, rearranging them if they start to char. Transfer the drumsticks to indirect medium heat. Cover the grill and cook until the juices run clear and the meat is no longer pink, 35 to 45 minutes more. For even cooking, rearrange them as needed, turning once or twice, while they cook.

⟶∘❯ STUBB GOES TO HOLLYWOOD

Joe Ely shares one of Stubb's classic tales, about Eddie Fisher. Eddie Fisher (dubbed the Jewish Sinatra) was one of Hollywood's most popular singers in the 1950s, and served in the army during the Korean conflict, where he met Sergeant C. B. Stubblefield. When Eddie Fisher abruptly left his wife Debbie Reynolds to marry their good friend Elizabeth Taylor in 1959, Hollywood ignited in scandal.

"After the war, Eddie Fisher invited Stubb to his place in Hollywood," says Joe. "So Stubb went out there, and this was right after Eddie Fisher married Elizabeth Taylor. Stubb stayed in an upstairs bedroom, in a house that he said 'was way too big for those people.' It wasn't anything personal about that house, he just felt it was just way too big for any two people.

"Stubb said, 'I was in a bedroom all the way down the hall, and I heard this woman screamin' and yellin' like she was really mad. So I got up and went to see if there was anything I could do to help.' And Stubb immediately understood they were havin' this ragin' fight. Elizabeth Taylor glared at Stubb and said, 'Who's that son-of-a-bitch?!'

Stubb says, 'I took one look at that woman—that was not a very nice woman.' He recommended that Eddie Fisher get rid of that woman as soon as possible. So Elizabeth Taylor throws Stubb out of the house, and he says, 'You know, there was just too much misery in that house for me anyway. I was glad to get outta there.'"

Stubb had been given a real bite of Hollywood, and it didn't taste good. Eddie Fisher waited a few years but eventually heeded Stubb's advice: His marriage to Elizabeth Taylor collapsed, and they divorced in 1964 when Taylor ran off with Richard Burton.

Seafood, from the River to the Gulf

"Barbecue" Skillet Shrimp

Sometimes, when the weather wasn't cooperating, Stubb would head indoors and "barbecue" some good, plump Texas Gulf Coast shrimp. He'd mix his sauce with lime juice, garlic, and a whole stick of butter, to make a shrimp dish that's simple but succulent. Eat these shrimp with your fingers (it's okay to suck the sauce right off the shells).

—●➤ SERVES 2 AS A MAIN COURSE, OR 4 AS AN APPETIZER

1 pound large shrimp, with shells
8 tablespoons salted butter (1 stick)
4 large cloves garlic, chopped
½ cup water
¼ cup prepared barbecue sauce
3 tablespoons freshly squeezed lime juice
½ teaspoon paprika
1 scallion (green and white parts), chopped
Warm crusty bread

1. Prepare the shrimp by pulling off the legs and, if desired, devein, but leave the shells on.
2. In a large skillet, melt the butter over medium heat. Stir in the garlic and cook until it just starts to soften, about 1 minute. Stir in the water, barbecue sauce, lime juice, and paprika. Bring to a boil, then reduce the heat and cook at a low boil (with bubbles gently but constantly breaking the entire surface), stirring occasionally, until the liquid thickens and no longer seems "watery," about 7 minutes.
3. Add the shrimp and raise the heat to medium-high. Cook, stirring often, until the shrimp shells are pink and the shrimps curl slightly, about 5 minutes. (Test one to see if it the meat is firm but not dry, and slips out of the shells easily.)
4. Sprinkle the scallion over the shrimp and serve hot, directly from the skillet, with crusty bread for mopping up the sauce.

Grilled Cornmeal Trout Fillets

You don't have to fry fish to get a crispy cornmeal coating—this recipe shows how to grill it instead. When spritzed with nonstick spray, the cornmeal grills up light and crisp, and helps prevent the fish from sticking to the grill. You can also pan-fry the fillets in a shallow layer of hot vegetable oil, about 2 minutes per side.

—◦⇒ SERVES 4 TO 6

½ cup yellow cornmeal
4 teaspoons barbecue seasoning or rub
4 teaspoons ground cumin
1 teaspoon salt
4 rainbow or steelhead trout, dressed and halved to make
    8 fillets
2 limes or 1 lemon, halved
Nonstick spray
Lime or lemon wedges (optional)

1. Prepare a grill for direct cooking (see page xix). For a charcoal grill, when the coals are ashed over, rake or spread them out in the bottom of the grill so the food can cook directly over the coals. (For a gas grill, fire up the burners so the food can cook directly over the heat.)

2. Mix together the cornmeal, barbecue seasoning, cumin, and salt in a shallow dish or pie pan. Set out a baking sheet (lined with foil for easy clean up, if desired).

3. Place the fillets on a work surface, skin side down. Squeeze just enough citrus juice over the fleshy side to penetrate, then flip the trout over and squeeze some juice over the skin side. Let the trout rest for at least 5 and up to 30 minutes to absorb the juice.

4. With paper towels, blot any excess moisture from the fillets. Lightly coat both sides of each fillet with the cornmeal mixture by placing them down flat in the mixture, then flipping them over. As you coat the fillets, set them skin side down on the baking sheet, then carry them out to the grill. (You can coat the trout up to 30 minutes before cooking.)

5. Generously spritz the fleshy side of the fillets with nonstick spray. Carefully place them over direct high heat, flesh side down. Cook until the coating crisps and shows grill marks, about 2 minutes.

6. Carefully lift the fillets and place them cooked side down on the baking sheet. Spray the uncooked side with nonstick spray. Set them back on the grill with the uncooked side down. Cook another few minutes, until the coating is crisp and the flesh cooked through (when probed with the tip of a knife, the flesh should just barely flake). Do not overcook or the trout will be dry. Serve with citrus wedges on the side.

Side Dishes and Salads

Rich 'n' Creamy Potato Salad

Stubb always said, "Potato salad is just like the Gulf Coast, the Brazos River, and the Colorado: It makes up Texas." He also said there are a million ways to make potato salad. This one is creamy, tangy with lemon and mustard, and chock full of pickles, red onion, and hard-cooked egg.

—⟶⟫ SERVES 6 TO 8

2 pounds russet potatoes (3 to 4 medium potatoes), rinsed
4 large eggs
1 tablespoon plus 1 teaspoon salt
¾ cup mayonnaise
¼ cup freshly squeezed lemon juice
(about 2 lemons' worth)
2 tablespoons Dijon mustard
2 tablespoons olive oil
¼ teaspoon granulated garlic or garlic powder
1½ cups finely diced dill pickles
1 cup finely diced red onion
2 tablespoons minced fresh parsley
Freshly ground pepper, to taste
Paprika for garnish

1. If the potatoes are large, quarter them. Place the potatoes and eggs (gently) in a large pot with 1 tablespoon of the salt and add water to cover by 1 inch. Bring to a boil over medium-high heat. Set a timer for 12 minutes. Reduce the heat until the water just simmers. When the timer goes off, scoop out the eggs with a slotted spoon and plunge them into a bowl of ice and water. (This prevents the yolks from turning green and makes peeling easier.) Continue to simmer the potatoes until they're easily pierced with a skewer, 20 to 30 minutes more. Drain the potatoes in a colander in the sink.
2. While the potatoes cook, combine ½ cup of the mayon-

naise, the lemon juice, mustard, olive oil, and garlic in a large mixing bowl.

3. When the potatoes are cool enough to handle but still warm, slip off and discard their skins and chop the potatoes into bite-size pieces. Combine the warm potatoes with the mixture in the bowl. Stir in the pickles, red onion, and parsley.

4. Shell the eggs and coarsely chop them, then add to the potatoes with the remaining ¼ cup of mayonnaise, the teaspoon of salt, and pepper. Taste and adjust the seasonings. Garnish with paprika and serve at room temperature or slightly chilled. Before serving, refresh the flavors as needed.

──◦❧ FEEDING THE SOULS AT ANTONE'S

"Behind Antone's blues club ran a gravel alleyway. Stubbs put his pit in this alley, and built a small shack around the pit for 'security' but it was generally left unlocked. Drifters down on their luck spent a lot of time in that alley, drinking wine from bags and selling their blood at the plasma center down the street. Smokin' barbecue on an unlocked pit is a drifter's delight, so we lost quite a bit of meat to them. Deep down, I don't think Stubb really cared. Then, one afternoon, Stubb caught one of them red-handed, taking a brisket right off the pit. I was sitting inside doing homework, when Stubb burst in the back door dragging one of the thieves in by his ear, yelling "Don't you ever steal from Stubb! If you're hungry, I'll feed you!" Stubb turned to me and said, "Rob, make this man the biggest plate of barbecue you can, and charge it to Stubb!" Stubb wasn't satisfied until I'd piled five pounds of meat on a paper plate. He handed it to the man and sent him back out into the alley. After that day, we never had any meat stolen from the pit, and only occasionally did any of the drifters take Stubb up on his offer to feed them."

—ROB PEARLMAN, who worked at Stubb's temporary barbecue
setup in Antone's (and who will never forget Stubb's words,
"Rob, go out and mop Johnny Cash's goat.")

Lemon-Pepper Cole Slaw

Know how to prevent watery, soggy cole slaw? Don't dress the cabbage until just before serving. You can make the dressing in advance, and shred the cabbage in advance, but wait until you're close to eating before you mix 'em together.

⟶◦≫ SERVES 6

3 scallions (green and white parts), finely chopped
Grated zest from 1 whole lemon
2 tablespoons freshly squeezed lemon juice
  (squeeze after zesting the lemon)
¼ cup buttermilk
½ cup mayonnaise
½ teaspoon salt
½ teaspoon coarse ground pepper
1 pound green cabbage, cored and finely shredded

1. Into a jar, measure and add all of the ingredients except the cabbage. Seal with the lid and shake to combine. (Or mix together in a bowl.) The dressing may be made a day in advance; refrigerate until ready to use. It will last up to a week in the refrigerator, but the flavors are freshest within a day.

2. Toss the cabbage with the dressing just before serving.

Stubb's Cole Slaw

Stubb's Restaurant in Austin adds a colorful Texas touch to their popular cole slaw by topping it with red cabbage and carrot shreds. But even without the garnishes, this slaw stands alone as a perfect complement to barbecue, grilled meats, and even sandwiches.

—◦❯❯ SERVES 4

¼ *cup very finely chopped white onion*
¼ *cup rice vinegar*
¼ *cup mayonnaise*
¼ *teaspoon freshly ground black pepper*
½ *teaspoon sugar*
½ *small head green cabbage*
Salt, to taste
½ *cup shredded red cabbage, for garnish (optional)*
½ *cup shredded carrot, for garnish (optional)*

1. Measure the onion, vinegar, mayonnaise, pepper, and sugar into a jar and shake to combine (or mix together in a small bowl). Refrigerate, covered, for up to 2 days.

2. Slice the green cabbage into very thin shreds. Toss with the dressing. Season with salt. Sprinkle the red cabbage and carrot shreds on top (if using), and serve.

Summertime Macaroni Salad

Stubb sang the blues classic "Summertime" all year long. It became his theme song. He'd sing "Summertime" when he was writing a letter to a friend, taking a shower, and always when he cooked. He'd make macaroni salad all year long, too, and naturally he'd sing his theme song when he made it. Hence the name of this dish: Summertime Macaroni Salad, but don't just make it for summer. The orange cheese, yellow corn, and green peppers in it make this salad a colorful addition to any seasonal table.

A few helpful tips: Cooked pasta absorbs the dressing better when warm. Chilling mutes flavors, so refresh them by stirring in more dressing ingredients, salt, pepper, and herbs, as needed just before serving. And finally, dice the ingredients small, about the size of shelled peanuts. The pasta and any mixins should be balanced, so you taste each ingredient in every mouthful.

——◦≫ SERVES 6 TO 8

8 ounces small pasta (such as elbows, medium shells,
   or other salad size)
¾ cup mayonnaise, preferably Hellman's® or Best Foods®
3 tablespoons freshly squeezed lemon juice
   (plus more as needed for refreshing)
1 tablespoon extra-virgin olive oil
½ cup minced onion
½ cup diced green bell pepper
1½ cups corn kernels (see Note)
4 ounces diced sharp Cheddar or longhorn cheese
   (about 1 cup)
½ teaspoon dried dill weed (optional)
½ teaspoon salt
¼ teaspoon freshly ground black pepper

1. Cook the pasta in a large pot with plenty of salted water until "al dente," according to package directions. Do not overcook. (You can chop the other ingredients while the water boils and the pasta cooks.)

2. Drain the pasta but do not rinse. Spoon the mayonnaise into a large bowl. While the pasta is warm, add it to the bowl and mix it up with the mayonnaise. Stir in the lemon juice and olive oil. Add the onion, bell pepper, and corn and mix. Finally, now that the pasta has cooled, mix in the cheese, dill, salt, and pepper. Serve at room temperature, or lightly chilled. Just prior to serving, taste the salad and refresh the flavors as needed. It may need more lemon juice, mayonnaise, salt, or pepper.

NOTE • For the corn, an 11-ounce can of Green Giant Niblets, when drained, yields 1½ cups, perfect for this recipe. A larger can (15½ ounces) yields up to 2 cups of drained corn, and that's fine too. Or use fresh corn (1 to 2 ears), or thawed frozen corn.

—◦✈ THE JUKEBOX

Some folks came to eat barbecue. Others came for the jukebox.
Legend has it that guitarist Stevie Ray Vaughan learned to
play Tin Pan Alley by listening to it on Stubb's jukebox. Here are
a few other tunes from that vintage music machine:

"Stand By"—John Lee Hooker
"A Change Is Gonna Come"—Sam Cooke
"If You Talk in Your Sleep"—Little Milton
"Superstition"—Stevie Wonder
"Stormy Monday Blues"—Bobby "Blue" Bland
"Tuff Enuff"—The Fabulous Thunderbirds
"Let It Shine"—Al Green
"I Hate to See You Leave"—Lightnin' Slim
"My Bow-Legged Woman"—Chuck Willis
"Born with the Blues"—Memphis Slim
"St. James Infirmary"—Warren Ceasar
"Mr. Charlie"—Lightnin' Hopkins
"Musta Notta Gotta Lotta"—Joe Ely
"Take the Bitter with the Sweet"—Muddy Waters
"Everyone Wants to Go to Heaven"—Albert King
"Who Do You Love?"—George Thorogood
"Why I Sing the Blues"—B. B. King
"It's Too Late"—Wilson Pickett
"Don't Be Cruel"—Elvis
"Sugar Hips"—Louisiana Red
"Only Time Will Tell"—Etta James
"Baby, What You Want Me to Do"—Little Richard
"Cold Cold Feeling"—T-Bone Walker
"Drivin' Wheel"—Albert King
"San-Ho-Zay"—Freddy King
"I'm Leavin' You"—Howlin' Wolf
"Hound Dog"—Big Mama Thornton
"Johnny B. Good"—Chuck Berry

Green Beans and Pecan Vinaigrette

When green beans are fresh and at their best, scoop up a pound for this dish: a lemony salad of vibrant, barely cooked green beans and crunchy toasted pecan halves. This salad is made in three quick stages (blanching the beans, toasting the nuts, and mixing the dressing), and each one can be prepared up to a day or two before serving. When you're ready to eat, simply toss the three elements together and serve. It's a good take-along salad: take it to a cookout, a tailgate, a picnic, or a potluck. Or just take it to the dinner table. Whether it's invited to a fancy affair or a casual buffet, this salad always makes friends.

—◦≫ SERVES 4

1 pound fresh green beans, trimmed and cut into 1½ to 2-inch
  lengths
1 cup shelled pecan halves
1 tablespoon corn oil or vegetable oil
¼ teaspoon salt
Freshly ground black pepper to taste

LEMON VINAIGRETTE

¾ teaspoon sugar
⅛ teaspoon salt, or to taste
1½ teaspoons Dijon mustard
2 tablespoons plus 1 teaspoon freshly squeezed lemon juice
⅓ cup corn oil or vegetable oil
3 tablespoons walnut oil or other oil for salads

1. Blanch the green beans by cooking them in a large pot of boiling salted water (about 3 quarts water and 1 teaspoon salt) just long enough to take the rawness out of them, but leave them crisply tender, 2 to 3 minutes. Scoop out the beans with a slotted spoon and plunge them into a large bowl of ice water, to stop the cooking. When completely cool, drain well in a colander. Chill the beans until ready to use. At this point they may be refrigerated for up to 2 days before use.

2. Cook the pecans in a skillet over medium heat, with the corn oil and salt, stirring often, for 8 to 10 minutes; watch them carefully because they can burn quickly. When they look like they *might* be done soon, take them off the heat, scoop them out of the pan, and let them cool. The hot nuts will continue to cook as they cool.

3. To make the Lemon Vinaigrette, measure the sugar, salt, mustard, and lemon juice into a jar, seal with a lid, and shake to dissolve the sugar and salt. Add the oils, seal, and shake furiously until the mixture is emulsified (blended completely, without separating).

4. Pour the beans into a serving bowl (pat them dry with paper towels if they're damp). Toss with the dressing (use only what you think you need) and the pecans. Season with salt and pepper as needed. Serve at room temperature.

"Potato salad is like the Gulf Coast, Brazos, and Colorado rivers—it makes up Texas."

—C. B. STUBBLEFIELD

Asiago-Scallion Bread

Bread and barbecue just seem to go together. This buttered-up loaf is as easy as garlic bread, with a fresh, tasty twist of sliced scallions, also known as green onions. Prepare it in advance, wrap it in foil, and when ready, heat it up. You can also warm it in a grill, over indirect heat, for great results.

—◦⋙ MAKES 1 LOAF; SERVES 6

1 (1-pound) loaf French or Italian bread
3 or 4 scallions (green and white parts), chopped
¼ pound (1 stick) softened butter
¼ cup grated Asiago or Romano cheese, or ½ cup shredded
2 teaspoons basil-flavored oil (optional)

1. Preheat the oven to 400°F.

2. Slice the loaf diagonally into ¾-inch wide slices. Tear off a piece of foil about 10 inches longer than the loaf and set it on a baking sheet. Place the loaf on the foil.

3. In a bowl, with a fork, blend together the scallions, butter, cheese, and oil (if using).

4. Open the bread slices like the pages of a book and spread the butter mixture on each slice, with a little on the top of the loaf as well. Loosely form the sides of the foil up around the loaf, leaving the top exposed. Bake in the oven for about 10 minutes, until the butter has melted and the top is brown. Serve in the foil, wrapped in a towel to keep warm.

Stubb's Sweet Corn Relish

Stubb always said to dice the chopped ingredients "small"—about twice the size of the corn kernels—for this sweet and tart relish. Unlike canned corn relishes, this version is uncooked, so the veggies stay crisp. It will last up to a week refrigerated, but you'll probably eat it all up long beforehand.

—❧ MAKES 3 TO 4 CUPS

1½ cups sweet corn (cut from 2 ears of corn),
*   or use thawed frozen corn*
½ cup diced red onion
½ cup diced white onion
1 cup diced peeled, seeded cucumber
½ cup diced red bell pepper
½ cup diced green bell pepper
¼ cup freshly squeezed lime juice (from 2 to 3 limes)
2 tablespoons white wine vinegar
2 tablespoons extra-virgin olive oil
1 teaspoon ground cumin
1 teaspoon sugar
⅛ teaspoon salt, or to taste
1 minced jalapeño, seeds and stem removed (optional)
Tabasco or other hot sauce, to taste (optional)

1. In a large bowl, combine the corn, onions, cucumber, and bell peppers. In a small bowl, mix together the lime juice, vinegar, oil, cumin, sugar, and salt until the sugar dissolves, then pour the dressing over the veggies. Mix everything together well, along with the jalapeño and Tabasco (if using).

2. Cover and chill at least 1 hour before serving, for the flavors to blend. Stir the mixture before serving.

SUGGESTION • Use the relish as a fancy, colorful salad dressing, tossing it with baby spinach or arugula leaves.

Jalapeño-Cheddar Corn Bread

Stubb said barbecue was "makin' do with what you got." In fact, he lived his whole life that way. When Stubb was in Korea, he cooked chili on the hot tailpipe of an army tank. He grew his own tomatoes there, too. And when Mess Sergeant Stubb managed to get his hands on cornmeal, he'd turn it into real Texas cornbread, an authentic taste of home for his fellow soldiers.

Stubb was also a practical man. In this recipe, to save washing another bowl, you can measure and mix the liquid ingredients in a 2-cup glass measuring cup, then pour the whole thing into the bowl of dry ingredients.

—•≫ MAKES ONE 7 X 11-INCH PAN

1¼ cups yellow cornmeal
¾ cup unbleached or all-purpose flour
1 tablespoon sugar
1 teaspoon baking soda
½ teaspoon salt
1 cup buttermilk (regular or low-fat)
⅓ cup corn oil or vegetable oil
2 large eggs
1 (15-ounce) can cream-style corn
2 jalapeños, stemmed, seeded, and finely chopped
   (or use pickled)
1 cup grated Cheddar cheese
Paprika for garnish

1. Preheat the oven to 350°F. Grease a 7 x 11-inch baking dish (or equivalent).

2. Combine the cornmeal, flour, sugar, baking soda, and salt in a large mixing bowl and stir well.

3. Measure the buttermilk into a 2-cup measuring cup, measure the oil on top of it, then add the eggs. Beat the eggs into the liquids with a fork. Pour the liquids, creamed corn, jalapeños, and ½ cup of the cheese into the cornmeal mixture. Stir just until mixed. (Do not overbeat, or the bread will be tough.) Pour the batter into the prepared baking dish. Sprinkle on the remaining ½ cup of cheese and the paprika. Bake for 35 to 40 minutes, until a toothpick poked in the center comes out clean. Cool slightly, slice into squares, and serve.

—◦⟫ SURPRISE PERFORMANCE

"*One afternoon at Stubb's first Austin restaurant, a couple of guys started bringing in sound equipment and setting it up on stage. Stubb gave them a puzzled look, but they just said someone paid them to set up a system and that person would be along shortly. Stubb and I sat there scratching our heads when a big bus pulled up, and in through the front door busted a smiling George Thorogood in his leopard-print coat. 'What's up, Pops? I'm hungry,' was all he said. In a flash, Stubb was pumping George's hand and fixing him a big ole plate of 'Cue. I knew we had a real scene about to happen, so I got out my phone book and called every musician I knew, and had them call everyone else. In one hour, the joint was packed to the rafters with two hundred folks. It was a great night. George played an entire set by himself on the acoustic guitar and sang a bunch of ancient country and western songs. That was just bizarre. Then his band walked in and they played for another hour. It was a great gift to Stubb from one of his true barbecue fans and friends.*"

—DEE PURKEYPILE,

who managed the weekly jams,

both in Lubbock and Austin

Bacon-Wrapped Green Bean Bundles

Maple syrup and bacon dress up these festive little bundles with almost no effort. Simply blanch the beans, bundle them in a bacon strip, and bake in a smoky maple-soy dressing. They're a fine complement to Wicked Chimichurri Wings (page 44), Tender Brined Pork Loin Chops (page 13), and Cider-Brined Turkey Breast (page 52).

—◦≫ SERVES 3 TO 4

¾ pound fresh green beans, trimmed
¼ cup maple syrup
1 tablespoon soy sauce
¼ to ½ teaspoon liquid smoke (optional)
5 strips thin-sliced bacon
¼ teaspoon freshly ground black pepper

1. Preheat the oven to 400°F.

2. Blanch the green beans in a large pot of boiling salted water (about 3 quarts water and 1 teaspoon salt) for 3 minutes. Drain in a colander and set under cold running water until cooled.

3. In a small bowl, combine the syrup, soy sauce, and liquid smoke (if using). Cut the bacon slices in half crossways.

4. Group the beans into 10 bundles of equal size. Wrap a piece of bacon around each bundle, overlapping the ends of the bacon. Arrange the bundles in a large baking dish, with the overlapping ends facing up, staggering the bundles as needed to fit in the pan.

5. Bake for 20 to 25 minutes, until the bacon starts to brown. Spoon the sauce over each bundle and sprinkle on the pepper. Continue baking for another 10 minutes, or until the beans are slightly wrinkled, the bacon lightly browned, and the sauce bubbles gently around the pan edges. Serve 2 to 3 bundles per person, with a bit of the pan juices spooned on top.

Serrano Pepper–Cheese Spinach

This stuff is rich! Which may be why it's one of the favorite side dishes at Stubb's Restaurant. It's kind of like a rebellious creamed spinach, tart with cream cheese and spicy with chiles, and pairs as well with fried chicken as it does with barbecue. Serrano peppers are sold in cans and jars, packed in a vinegar brine. Feel free to chop up the carrots that come packed with them.

—◦⟫ SERVES 4 TO 6

1 pound frozen chopped spinach
8 ounces cream cheese, cut into chunks
¼ cup heavy whipping cream
¼ cup chopped pickled serranos
1 tablespoon minced garlic
1 teaspoon salt
¾ teaspoon freshly ground black pepper

1. Cook the spinach according to package directions (do not overcook). Drain well in a colander. Press out excess water with the back of a spoon or a spatula.
2. Place the cream cheese, cream, serranos, garlic, salt, and pepper in a medium saucepan. Add the spinach and stir over medium-low heat until the cream cheese melts. When all the ingredients are evenly combined and the mixture is warm, serve.

Grilled Potato Planks

Grill these zesty potato slices until they're soft in the center and golden brown on the outside. They're best eaten hot, right off the grill—and that's when half of them disappear. Large potato slices are less likely to slip through the grates.

——◦≫ SERVES 4

2 pounds large russet (baking) potatoes
¼ cup corn oil or vegetable oil
1 tablespoon dried marjoram or Italian seasoning
2 tablespoons lemon-pepper seasoning salt

1. Scrub the potatoes and pat dry. Do not peel. Slice the potatoes lengthwise into ¼-inch-thick pieces.

2. Pour the oil into a rimmed baking sheet. Push the potato slices around in the oil, turning to coat all sides. Crush the herbs between your fingers as you sprinkle them over both sides of the potatoes. Let the potatoes rest in the herbs from 15 minutes to 1 hour. Sprinkle with lemon-pepper seasoning just before cooking, so it doesn't draw out the juices from the potatoes.

3. Prepare a grill for direct cooking (see page xix). For a charcoal grill, when the coals are ashed over, rake or spread them out in the bottom of the grill so the food can cook directly over the coals. (For a gas grill, fire up the burners so the food can cook directly over the heat.)

4. Over direct medium-high heat, grill the potatoes on one side until golden brown, then flip over and grill the other side. The potatoes are done when crisp and browned on the outside but tender in the center, 10 to 15 minutes total cooking time. Serve hot off the grill. If not serving immediately, tent with foil; they'll soften but still be tasty, or recrisp them on a hot grill just before serving.

Stubb's Restaurant Pintos

Stubb cooked his pinto beans the same way he did his brisket: low and slow. By adding only as much water as the beans can absorb, in three stages, you'll end up with classic creamy beans, coated in a thick, bacon-rich broth. His tips: No soaking and no long boiling, just a bare simmer and an occasional stir. (The exact amount of water and cooking time varies depending on the age of the beans.) The restaurant serves his beans plain, but some folks like to top them with extra flavorings, like chopped onion, cilantro, or shredded cheese.

—◦≫ SERVES 8

1 pound dried pinto beans
3 strips bacon, finely chopped
½ large onion, finely chopped
1 tablespoon chopped garlic
1 teaspoon finely chopped jalapeño
1 teaspoon dried oregano
1 teaspoon ground cumin
½ teaspoon freshly ground black pepper
1½ teaspoons salt
Chopped onion, cilantro, and grated cheese, for garnish
(optional)

1. Pick through the beans to discard any pebbles or other debris. Rinse the beans well and drain.

2. In a heavy pot, brown the bacon over medium-high heat. Stir in the onion, garlic, jalapeño, oregano, cumin, and pepper. Cook, stirring often, until the onion softens, another 2 minutes or so.

3. Add the beans and pour in 6 cups of water or enough to cover the beans by 1 inch. Bring the beans to a boil, then reduce the heat so that the beans cook at a bare simmer. Do not cover the pot. Slowly simmer the beans, without stirring, until the beans start to poke through the liquid, about 45 minutes. Stir the beans up from the bottom, add 2 cups water, and simmer, without stirring, until the beans poke through the liquid again, about 30 minutes more.

4. Stir in another ½ cup water and continue simmering. When the beans are almost tender, after 10 to 20 minutes, stir in the salt. (If the beans still seem hard in the center, add a little more water and simmer longer.) Simmer the beans to absorb the salt and until the beans are tender, about 5 minutes more; the beans are done when the liquid is creamy and the beans are cooked through but still have some texture. Total cooking time is usually 1½ to 2 hours. Serve the beans and their creamy broth in small bowls or cups, adding garnishes (such as onions, cilantro, or cheese) as desired.

> **"They build barb wire fences around old locomotives. I'll be damn if they do that to me."**
>
> **—C. B. STUBBLEFIELD**

Black-Eyes 'n' Bacon

Slow-cooked beans take on a fresh attitude with one tiny extra step: Fry up sliced bacon and diced vegetables for simmering with the beans. But before adding the beans, save half the mixture and stir it into portions just before serving. The slightly crisp peppers, celery, and bacon pieces add contrast to the soft creaminess of the beans, while the longer cooked bacon and vegetables give up their flavors to the overall dish. For extra punch, splash on a bit of olive oil and vinegar at table.

SERVES 8 TO 10

1 pound dried black-eyed peas or other beans
½ pound thick-sliced smoked bacon, cut into ¼-inch-wide
   pieces
1 medium onion, cut into small dice
2 ribs celery, cut into small dice
½ red bell pepper, cut into small dice
½ green bell pepper, cut into small dice
4 cloves garlic, minced
2 to 3 teaspoons salt, or to taste
½ teaspoon freshly ground black pepper
Olive oil and wine vinegar (optional)

1. Pick through the beans to discard any pebbles or other debris. Rinse the beans well. Soak in plenty of water to cover for at least 4 hours or overnight. Drain the beans and set aside.
2. In a heavy pot, fry the bacon over medium-high heat until it browns, about 10 minutes. Stir in the onion, celery, bell peppers, and garlic and cook, stirring occasionally, until the vegetables soften but still have some crispness, about 5 minutes. Scoop out half the mixture and set aside (refrigerate if you're not planning to serve the beans as soon as they're cooked.)
3. Add the beans to the remaining vegetables in the pot and enough water to cover by 1 inch (6 to 8 cups). Bring to a boil

over high heat, then reduce the heat so the beans slowly simmer. Do not cover the pot. Start testing after 20 minutes, though they make take as long as 1 hour. When the beans start to feel soft, stir in the salt and pepper. Stir the beans occasionally as they cook; they're done when just tender, but not mushy. (Note: For a thicker bean broth, puree ½ to 1 cup of the beans and return them to the pot.)

4. Ladle the beans, with some of their liquid, into bowls or cups. Spoon on some of the reserved bacon mixture (reheat if necessary in skillet or microwave). For extra flavor, drizzle with olive oil and a splash of vinegar to taste.

⟶◦⟫ FOOD TRUMPS COLOR

Everyone who knew him said Stubb was colorblind. "Black, white, green, red. He didn't care what color you were. People were just people to him," says his daughter Doris.

In 1970s Texas, though, not everyone shared that attitude. Even folks who weren't prejudiced were keenly aware of the written and unwritten rules about race. It was just something that hung in the air, like dust from a West Texas tornado.

Stubb had a knack for putting away the race issue as soon as it came up. Once, two elderly white ladies stuck their heads in his door and asked, "Do you serve white women here?"

"Nah," he replied. "We can't fit 'em on the plate."

Another time, a Latino worker cautiously asked, "Do you serve Mexicans?"

"No, sir!" Stubb snapped back. "We serve brisket, ribs, and beans!"

He'd then flash his wide, inviting grin, and proudly serve them the best barbecue in West Texas, and possibly beyond.

Mashed Sweet Potatoes, Stubb's Style

When boiling sweet potatoes, don't cut them up first—they take on too much liquid and taste watered down. If the sweet potatoes are too large to fit in the pan, then you'll have to cut them in half, but try to buy ones that aren't too big. At Stubb's Restaurant in Austin, these sweet gems come mashed with a sprinkling of toasted pecans on top.

—◦» SERVES 4 TO 6

2 pounds whole sweet potatoes
1½ teaspoons salt
3 tablespoons unsalted butter
⅓ to ½ cup dark brown sugar (depends on how sweet you
    like 'em)
⅓ cup heavy cream
½ teaspoon vanilla extract
Toasted pecan pieces, for garnish (optional)

1. Rinse the sweet potatoes but don't peel them, and halve them only if they're too large to fit in the pot. Place them in a large pot with 1 teaspoon of the salt and enough water to cover them by 1 inch. Boil the sweet potatoes until tender enough to be easily pierced with a skewer, 15 to 35 minutes. Drain them in a colander in the sink.
2. While the potatoes cool slightly, combine the butter, brown sugar, cream, vanilla, and remaining ½ teaspoon salt in a mixing bowl. Peel the warm potatoes (the jackets should slip right off), cut them into large chunks, and toss them in the bowl. Mash until the mixture is combined. Serve warm, garnished with pecan pieces (if using). The sweet potatoes may be refrigerated and reheated before serving.

SPICE IT UP • Mash in a dash of any of these warm spices for extra flavor: cinnamon, nutmeg, ground ginger, Chinese five-spice powder, allspice, cloves, or white pepper.

Stubb never intended to bottle his sauce. For years, his friends Sharon and Joe Ely begged him to do it, but he was too stubborn to agree. Then, around Christmas of 1989, Sharon tried a new strategy. "He needed money for Christmas presents, so I said, please let us do it just this once. We can sell the sauce for folks to give as gifts." This time, Stubb agreed.

Sharon and Stubb set to work in her home kitchen, just outside Austin. Stubb brought in enormous battered pots, old jam jars, and empty whiskey bottles. "We had tables end to end, all the way down the kitchen. Stubb and I sterilized the bottles, filled them, canned them, and tied them with little raffia strips. The kitchen was steaming hot, and we splattered barbecue sauce all over the walls, the floor, and the ceiling." With an old Apple computer, video camera, and a portrait of Stubb by Paul Milosevich, Joe printed up labels, which Stubb cut out with scissors.

The next step was a Christmas sight never to be forgotten. Sharon is a tall, strikingly pretty woman, with entrepreneurial flare. "We called a bunch of our friends, told them about Stubb's sauce, and took $150 in orders the very first day." Singer-songwriter Kimmie Rhodes, also from Lubbock, pitched in to help. Kimmie stands several hands shorter than Sharon. Donned in matching frilly, white formals, cowboy hats, and boots, the gals delivered the sauce—while a Stetson-capped Stubb slowly drove them door to door in his red-and-white Cadillac.

That first $150 was a real eye-opener for Stubb. "He couldn't believe he could make that much money just from selling his sauce," Sharon says. After New Year's, Stubb rented a warehouse in South Austin and commenced hand-bottling his sauce from there.

Of course every bottle looked different, because he was still sterilizing recycled whiskey bottles of every shape and size. But he liked the way they looked (especially the Crown Royals), and to this day, a few of the original, hand-filled, hand-labeled "Stubb's Bar-B-Que Sauce" still exist in the Austin area.

Desserts for Feelin' Good

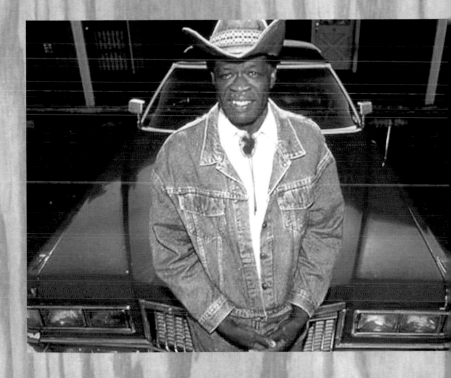

Stubb's Pecan Pie

Pecan pies in Texas are as plentiful as stars in the Lubbock sky. This is Stubb's original recipe, and it shines brightly among all the other pecan pie recipes. Don't be shy about doubling the recipe and baking two pies. The first one always seems to disappear.

—◦≫ MAKES 1 (9-INCH) PIE

1 unbaked 9-inch pie shell (fresh, frozen, or ready-to-cook)
1½ cups pecan halves (6 ounces)
3 large eggs
1 cup sugar
4 teaspoons vanilla extract
½ teaspoon salt
¾ cup dark corn syrup
4 tablespoons (½ stick) butter, melted

1. Preheat the oven to 350°F.

2. Set the pie shell on a baking sheet. Pour the pecans into the pie shell.

3. In a mixing bowl with a wire whisk, beat the eggs until well mixed, about 30 seconds. Mix in the sugar, vanilla, and salt. Whisk in the corn syrup and melted butter until everything's blended together.

4. Pour the filling over the pecans into the pie shell. Bake the pie (on the baking sheet) for 45 to 50 minutes, until the top puffs up and browns. If the crust darkens too quickly, shield it with a ring of foil for the last 15 minutes or so of cooking. Cool for 1 to 2 hours before serving.

Dark Caramel-Pecan Sauce

This simple sauce tastes like a spoonable version of dark cara-
mel candies, with the added crunch of toasted pecans. Spoon it
over vanilla-bean ice cream for a classic dessert. Or drizzle it
over grilled fruit kebabs, skewered with apples and bananas.
Karo brand makes a corn syrup version with brown sugar,
which is ideal for this recipe. As a variation, you may make the
sauce with light corn syrup and light brown sugar; it will be
more blonde in color and milder tasting. Pick your preference.

——⁂≫ MAKES 1 CUP

¾ cup packed dark brown sugar
⅓ cup corn syrup (see Headnote)
2 tablespoons butter
¼ plus ⅛ teaspoon salt
1 teaspoon vanilla extract
¼ cup toasted chopped pecans (see Note)
⅓ cup heavy whipping cream

1. Place the brown sugar, corn syrup, butter, and ¼ teaspoon
of the salt in a small saucepan over medium heat. Stir often as
the mixture comes to a boil, letting the sugar dissolve. When the
sauce boils, immediately reduce the heat to low and stir constantly until the sauce thickens slightly (to the consistency of
chocolate syrup), about 2 minutes. (Tips: Watch to make sure
the mixture doesn't boil over. Don't let it thicken too much, or as
it cools, it will harden into candy.) Stir in the vanilla and pecans.
Remove the pan from the heat and let the sauce cool slightly, 8
to 10 minutes.
2. While the sauce is still warm but not hot, stir in the cream
with a spatula. At first, the sauce (which has thickened even
more) may seem hard to stir, but keep at it until the cream
blends uniformly into the sauce, just a minute or so. Taste the
sauce; if desired, stir in the remaining ⅛ teaspoon salt. (Salt

Dark Caramel-Pecan Sauce (*continued*)

boosts the overall sweet-caramel flavor of the sauce, as long as you don't add too much, or too little.)

Serve the sauce warm, by reheating in a saucepan or microwave (use short bursts so it doesn't boil over), or serve it cold. Be sure to stir it before serving, as the nuts tend to float to the top. Store in the refrigerator up to 1 week.

NOTE • To toast nuts: For a small number of pecan pieces like this, you can easily toast them in a skillet over medium-low heat, shaking often, until light brown, 6 to 8 minutes. Watch them closely and take them off the heat just when they start to color, or they'll jump from toasted to burned in seconds.

> **"I guarantee you one thing, you ain't gonna cook no better than I can. Another thing, you not gonna love people no better than I can."**
>
> —C. B. STUBBLEFIELD

Stubb's Buttermilk Pie

Stubb always cooked up three pies at a time, for serving in the restaurant. This version, his original recipe, is scaled down to make a single pie. You can simply double or triple the ingredients to make two or three pies, if you like, and bake them on two racks, staggered for even cooking.

——⁕≫ MAKES 1 (9-INCH) PIE

1 unbaked 9-inch pie shell (fresh, frozen, or ready-to-cook)
⅔ cup granulated sugar
5 tablespoons softened butter or margarine
1 teaspoon vanilla extract
3 tablespoons all-purpose flour
¾ cup buttermilk
3 large eggs, beaten

1. Preheat oven to 350°F. Set the pie shell on a baking sheet.

2. In a mixing bowl, cream together the sugar, butter, and vanilla. Mix in the flour. Pour in the buttermilk and eggs, and whisk or beat until everything's blended together.

3. Pour the filling into the pie shell. Bake the pie (on the baking sheet) for 40 to 45 minutes, until the top puffs slightly and turns golden brown. (If the crust browns too quickly, shield it with a ring of foil for the last 10 minutes of cooking.) Cool for 30 to 60 minutes before serving warm, or store the cooled pie in the refrigerator until ready to serve.